Prosodic characteristics of
Orkney and Shetland dialects

An experimental approach

Published by
LOT
Trans 10
3512 JK Utrecht
The Netherlands

phone: +31 30 253 6006
fax: +31 30 253 6000
e-mail: lot@let.uu.nl
http://wwwlot.let.uu.nl/

Front cover: Standing stones of Stenness, Orkney. Photograph by Bram van den Berg.

ISBN 90-76864-57-8

NUR 632

Prosodic characteristics of Orkney and Shetland dialects

An experimental approach

PROEFSCHRIFT

ter verkrijging van
de graad van Doctor aan de Universiteit Leiden,
op gezag van de Rector Magnificus Dr. D.D. Breimer,
hoogleraar in de faculteit der Wiskunde en
Natuurwetenschappen en die der Geneeskunde,
volgens besluit van het College voor Promoties
te verdedigen op donderdag 23 september 2004
klokke 14.15

door

KLASKE VAN LEIJDEN

geboren te Gouda in 1959

Promotiecommissie

Table of contents

CONTENTS

CONTENTS

1   General introduction

1.1   Introduction

Vikings settled in Orkney and Shetland – north of mainland Scotland – in the
ninth century, possibly even earlier. The Norse language spoken by the
invaders and their descendants became known as 'Norrœna' or 'Norn', and it
all but obliterated the languages spoken by earlier inhabitants of the Isles.
Orkney and Shetland, collectively referred to as the Northern Isles, remained
part of the Scandinavian territory until 1468–9, when the islands were
pledged to Scotland as part of a dowry. Through Scottish government and
settlement in the Northern Isles, the Norn language was finally abandoned in
favour of Lowland Scots in the course of the eighteenth century.[1]

Present-day Orkney and Shetland dialects have several distinctive
features that can possibly be ascribed to the Norn substratum, for example,
the use of perfective *be* rather than *have*, as in *I'm seen him*; palatalisation of
initial /g/ and /k/ and, chiefly in Shetland, TH stopping, e.g. *den* for 'then'
and *eart* for 'earth'. (See Chapter 2 for a brief discussion of the main
characteristics of the two dialects.) In Shetland dialect, stressed monosyllables seem to have preserved their typically Scandinavian syllable
structure, such that phonetically long vowels are obligatory followed by
phonetically short consonants and short vowels by long consonants (Catford
1957a). Furthermore, according to popular belief, there are affinities in
intonation between Orkney, but not necessarily Shetland, speech and
varieties of Norwegian. In fact, there appears to be a striking dissimilarity in
intonation between the two dialects. Impressionistically, Orkney dialect is
characterised by a very distinctive, lilting, rise-fall intonation pattern, while
Shetland speech is relatively low pitched with a somewhat level intonation.

---

[1] The term (Lowland) Scots in this dissertation refers to the northern variety of
English spoken in Scotland to the east and south of the Highland Line; to the west of
this line, we find Gaelic and Highland English speakers.

The Norn language and its demise has been the subject of several studies (cf. Barnes 1989 and 1998 and references therein). The dialect vocabulary of Orkney and Shetland is well documented in the etymological dictionaries of Marwick (1929) and Jakobsen (1928/1932) respectively, as well as in the more popular dictionaries of Graham (1993) and Flaws and Lamb (1996). Catford (1957b) investigated the vowel system of Shetland speech and, more recently, Melchers (e.g. 1981, 1985) has examined language attitudes in Shetland. However, there appear to be no published works dealing with present-day Orkney dialect, nor are there any contrastive studies examining the linguistic structures of the dialects of the Northern Isles. In addition, it should be noted that nearly all relevant research has focused chiefly on the Scandinavian substratum of the two dialects and, because of this, our knowledge of Northern Isles Scots remains somewhat one-sided.

The first aim of the present study is to establish whether in Shetland dialect, durationally short consonants follow durationally long vowels and vice versa, and whether this feature is also found in Orkney dialect. Secondly, we will carry out a series of perception experiments investigating the role of intonation versus segmental information in the identification of Orkney and Shetland dialects by native listeners of each of these varieties. Thirdly, we will present a preliminary account of the characteristic features of the intonation systems of the two varieties. Finally, we investigated the perceptual relevance of the prosodic parameters that were identified in the acoustic investigation. The main objective of this investigation, therefore, is to conduct a contrastive examination of the prosodic structure of Orkney and Shetland dialects in order to establish if, and to what extent, the two dialects differ prosodically. Furthermore, we will try to determine if the observed prosodic characteristics can be ascribed to the Scandinavian substratum or if they should be attributed to Scottish influences.

To understand today's linguistic situation in the Northern Isles it is helpful to know something of the historical background. Chapter 2 provides a brief outline of the political and social developments that may have played a role in the linguistic divergence of the two island communities at issue. From this overview, it will become clear that the histories of Orkney and Shetland diverged at an early stage. Even so, Norn remained spoken in both island groups, increasingly, as time went by, alongside Lowland Scots, and died out in both places at about the same point.

1.2 The relationship between vowel and consonant duration

1.2.1 Vowel and consonant duration in Shetland dialect

Catford (1957a) points out that one of the most general characteristics of Shetland dialect that can most likely be ascribed to the Norn substratum is its 'Scandinavian' syllable structure. The essential feature of this is that in stressed monosyllabic words, a long vowel (V:) is always followed by a short consonant (C), and a short vowel (V) is followed by a long consonant (C:). So in Shetland dialect we find, for example, *bait* [be:t] versus *beat* [bet:]. This kind of inverse relationship between vowel and final consonant duration, which is usually referred to as 'complementary quantity' (cf. Elert 1964), is found in several Scandinavian languages. Yet it seems that, at least for Swedish, there is considerable dialectal variation with respect to the vowel/final-consonant ratios (Strangert 2001). Consonant duration is also reflected in Scandinavian spelling, for example as in Norwegian, *tak* [ta:k] 'roof, ceiling' versus *takk* [tak:] 'thanks'. The phenomenon is the result of the Great Scandinavian Quantity Shift that took place between 1250 and 1550 (Haugen 1976).[2]

In Lowland Scots and in Scottish Standard English (SSE) vowel duration is also predictable.[3] The Scottish Vowel Length Rule (SVLR), which is the result of a sixteenth-century sound change, predicts that, in monosyllabic words, a stressed vowel is phonetically short unless it is followed by a voiced fricative or /r/, in which case it is long. A vowel is also long if followed by a word or morpheme boundary, thus, we find *agree#d* /i:/ versus *need* /i/. The SVLR does not apply to the vowels /ɪ/ and /ʌ/, which are invariably short (Aitken 1981). Both the operation and the acquisition of the SVLR in SSE have recently been the subject of several studies (McClure 1977, Agutter 1987, McKenna 1988, Scobbie, Turk and Hewlett 1999, Hewlett, Matthews and Scobbie 1999). There appears to be as yet no published work focussing on the SVLR in rural Lowland Scots.

---

[2] Nevertheless, there are a number of Scandinavian (mostly Swedish) dialects where -VC (with both short V and C) has remained; also, dialects have been documented in which -V:C: syllables have been preserved (Haugen 1976, Strangert 2001).

[3] Scottish Standard English in this dissertation means standard (or near-standard) English spoken with what Abercrombie (1979) calls the basic Scottish vowel system, which has nine monophthongs /i e a ɔ ɔ ɪ u ɛ ʌ/ and three diphthongs /ai au ɔi/.

According to Árnason (1980:90–91) the most important difference between the SVLR and the Great Scandinavian Quantity Shift is that the main effect of the change in Scots has been a general shortening of long vowels, whereas the Scandinavian shift seems to have resulted in greater harmonisation of syllabic quantity. The importance one assigns to this difference depends on the criteria used. A typology based on the presence versus absence of free phonological length in vowels would put Scots in the same category as the Nordic languages, whereas a typology based on presence versus absence of fixed syllabic quantity would put Scots in the same category as English.

Returning to the Shetland dialect situation, Aitken (1981) observes that some apparent vowel length irregularities with contrastive effects do occur in Shetland dialect. In this variety, SVLR vowels before /d/ appear both with long and short realisations: [nid:] *need*, but [mi:d] *meid* 'meith, landmark', and [gød:] *good* but [bø:d] *böd* 'fishermen's booth'. The items with the long realisations all derive from earlier forms with the voiced fricative /ð/ as the syllable-closing consonant, i.e. one of the SVLR-long environments. Hence, once we know the etymology of a particular word, we are able to predict the vowel duration. In the lengthy introduction to his etymological dictionary, Jakobsen (1928/1932) does not discuss duration, although he uses double consonants in his spelling, and marks vowels for length.[4]

Melchers (1984) analysed recordings made during her own fieldwork, in addition to data collected in the Linguistic Survey of Scotland (published in Mather and Speitel 1975, 1977, 1986). She found that the SVLR generally applies to the collected material, and that durationally long vowels are found before /d/ derived from historical /ð/. She observed that, throughout the Linguistic Survey of Scotland, fieldworkers consistently marked consonant and vowel duration in monosyllables clearly following the –V:C or –VC: pattern, but that the occurrence of long consonants tended to be restricted chiefly to words of Scandinavian origin. However, she does not give any measurements to support her argument, neither does she give the context in which the words were pronounced, nor does she provide any information concerning the speakers. Therefore, it is somewhat difficult to draw convincing conclusions regarding the syllable structure of Shetland dialect, or to compare the findings to instrumental studies investigating the SVLR in other Scots dialects.

---

[4] According to Stewart (1964), Jakobsen's spelling is 'phonetics run riot'.

Like Shetland dialect, Orcadian, too, has a substantial Norn substratum. Yet, owing to the lack of studies investigating aspects of Orkney dialect, nothing is known about the relationship between vowel and final consonant duration in this variety.

[handwritten margin note: flags up a large gap in the dialect literature]

1.2.2 Research questions and approach

The aim of Chapter 3 is to establish whether in present-day Orkney and Shetland dialects durationally short consonants invariably follow durationally long vowels and vice versa; and if so, do we find such an inverse relationship throughout the vocabulary, or is it lexical-incidental and limited to Norn loanwords or words which are subject to the SVLR. To address these questions, we undertook a series of identical production experiments with speakers from Orkney and Shetland, using speakers of Scottish Standard English to provide a control condition. Furthermore, the outcome of the investigations will be evaluated against results obtained in similar experiments with speakers from Scandinavia.

[handwritten margin note: research Q]

[handwritten margin notes: Ork; (Shet; SSE (control) + Scand]

1.3 Intonation

1.3.1 Background

The linguistic literature dealing with the dialects of the Northern Isles generally focuses on Shetland, while Orkney is either dismissed briefly or ignored (cf. Aitken 1992, McClure 1994, Görlach 2002). It seems simply to be assumed that features found in Shetland speech also occur in Orkney and, consequently, the two dialects are generally believed to be one and the same. However, there seem to be striking differences between the dialects of Orkney and Shetland, especially with respect to speech melody. In fact, native Shetlanders typically claim that it is very easy to identify an Orcadian by his intonation alone.

[handwritten margin note: interesting]

There appear to be no published works investigating aspects of Orkney or Shetland intonation. Impressionistically, Shetland speech has a somewhat narrow pitch range and, with respect to intonation, Shetland dialect seems not dissimilar from mainland Lowland Scots, which, apart from the English spoken in the Glasgow conurbation, is characterised by sequences of falling tones, while rises of any sort are rare (Cruttenden 1997:136). Orcadian apparently does not fit this description. Orkney speech is characterised by a very distinctive, rise-fall intonation pattern, whereby the pitch rise seems to occur relatively late in the word and 'the curious lilting intonation is that of Norway, not of Scotland' (Marwick 1932:261).[5] Leaving aside for the moment what is meant by a 'Norwegian' melody, the question now arises as to why we should find such a melody in Orkney, but not in Shetland dialect, which, at least with respect to syllable structure (cf. Chapter 3), appears to be the more Scandinavian of the two varieties. Moreover, Orkney dialect is, even within Scotland, often mistaken for Welsh English, which also has frequent rise-fall intonation patterns and relatively late pitch peaks (Tench 1990, Cruttenden 1997:133). A similar extensive use of rising tones is reported for Glasgow, Liverpool (Cruttenden 1995) and Belfast (Jarman and Cruttenden 1976, Grabe 2002). What these varieties have in common is that all of them have been influenced either directly, or indirectly, by a Celtic language. Nevertheless, late pitch peaks have also been reported for a number of Germanic language varieties, such as Danish and Swedish (Grønnum 1990) as well as for Rhine Valley German (Gibbon 1996).

Regrettably, none of the authors of seventeenth and eighteenth-century journals comment on intonation, or on any linguistic differences between the dialects of Orkney and Shetland. Therefore, we are unable to tell whether the melodic differences observed today are relatively recent developments or if they date from the Viking era, when Norn was still spoken throughout the Northern Isles. Even so, in a brief article on Shetland dialect, Laurenson (1860) writes that there is a marked distinction between the dialects of Shetland on the one hand and Orkney and Caithness (see map, on p. 12) on the other, but we do not learn in what aspects the dialects may differ. The subject of intonation was also overlooked in Jakobsen's (1928/1932) and Marwick's (1929) standard works on the dialects. More recent travel writers appear to be more observant, for example, Bryson (1998:56) refers to the 'melodic rising intonation' of native Orcadians, while O'Hanlon (2003:19) speaks about Orkney's 'lilting ... gentle musical accent'.

1.3.2   The role of intonation in the identification of language varieties

Several experiments have been carried out in order to find evidence for the belief that language varieties can be identified solely on the basis of intonation. For instance, in order to establish whether subjects can distinguish between English, Japanese and Cantonese, Ohala and Gilbert

---

[5] Marwick, although a professional linguist and philologist, made this particular remark in a chapter that he contributed to a tourist guide.

(1980) converted speech fragments from these languages into a buzz, whilst preserving the amplitude and intonation contour of the original; later Schaeffler and Summers (1999) used low-pass filtered, i.e. unintelligible, speech, in order to demonstrate melodic differences between certain varieties of German. The investigators report a better-than-chance level of correct identification, particularly when dealing with one's own language variety.

Gooskens (1997) and Gooskens and van Bezooijen (2002) examined the importance of intonation versus segmental information to the identification of Dutch and English dialects by native speakers of these languages. Subjects were presented with three types of speech: (1) unintelligible (low-pass filtered) with the original intonation contour left intact 'intonation only', (2) intelligible and monotonised 'segmental information only' and (3) normal speech. The results of these experiments showed that segmental information consistently played a more important role than intonation in the recognition of regional varieties. Still, as correct dialect classification was well above chance for the 'intonation only' condition, it seems that the role of intonation cannot be completely ignored. Gooskens (to appear) examines the role of intonation in the identification of Norwegian dialects by Norwegian teenagers. Comparing the results for Norwegian with those obtained by Gooskens (1997) for Dutch, she finds that when intonation was removed from an utterance, dialect classification proves to be more difficult for Norwegian than for Dutch listeners.

In the experiments discussed so far, the role of intonation in the recognition of dialects was investigated by means of an elimination technique. However, when speech is monotonised, only the pitch contour is removed, whilst other prosodic cues, such as syllable and word boundaries, as well as differences in loudness between individual vowels, are maintained. Removal of segmental information by low-pass filtering destroys this crucial prosodic information. Therefore, the elimination method does not afford a straightforward comparison between the role of segmental features versus intonation in the identification of language varieties.

One way to overcome the aforementioned problem is to use segmental information from the standard variety of a language, and create different stimuli by superimposing intonation contours that are characteristic for specific dialects. Using such an experimental design, Gilles, Peters, Auer and Selting (2001) presented listeners with neutral carrier phrases recorded by a speaker of Standard German. One half of the set of utterances were given Hamburg intonation contours, while the other half retained the original intonation. Similarly, Peters, Gilles, Auer and Selting (2002) investigated the role of intonation in the recognition of Berlin German. In both cases, it was demonstrated that listeners are able to identify these particular varieties of German on the basis of pitch information alone.

The two methods – the elimination technique versus the use of neutral carrier phrases – have been evaluated by Peters, Gilles, Auer and Selting (2003). In their first experiment, Freiburg, Duisburg, Mannheim or Dresden contours were superimposed on speech fragments that had been converted into a schwa-like humming sound. Native listeners from Freiburg and Dresden were asked to assign each stimulus to one of the four varieties. For the second experiment, the same four regional contours were superimposed onto a recording of a male speaker of Standard German. It was found that when presented with unintelligible speech, i.e. the humming sound, both listener groups had moderate success in recognising their own language variety, but failed in the identification of any of the other varieties. This outcome is similar to the results reported by Gooskens (1997). However, when presented with Standard German carrier phrases with transplanted contours, both the Freiburg and the Dresden listeners performed considerably better, with identification rates significantly above chance for all four intonation conditions. Nevertheless, both listener groups performed best in recognising the intonation contour of their own language variety. The results produced by Peters et al. (2003) indicate that, at least for German listeners, using neutral segmental information – rather than unintelligible speech lacking crucial prosodic information – enhances dialect recognition rates.

In a study guided primarily by pedagogical considerations, Willems (1982) explored non-native intonation. He reported a number of perceptual investigations, using intelligible as well as unintelligible speech, whereby pitch contours were systematically manipulated in order to test the acceptability of these contours to native speakers of English. It was shown that linguistically naive English listeners were quite capable of judging the acceptability of native language contours.

To summarise, it has been variously demonstrated that listeners are well able to recognise languages or dialects solely on the basis of melodic information, particularly when identifying their own language variety. However, the presence of other prosodic cues, such as syllable and word boundaries, considerably improves performance.

1.3.3   Research issues and approach

The chief aim of Chapters 4, 5 and 6 is to investigate the validity of impressionistic claims that there are intonational differences between the dialects of Orkney and Shetland. To begin with, we will examine the role of intonation versus segmental information in the identification of Orkney and Shetland dialects by native listeners of each of these varieties. We will then carry out an acoustic investigation of the prosodic structure of the two dialects. Finally, the relevance of the established prosodic parameters will be evaluated perceptually. To address these issues, we will carry out a series of experiments using a combination of the methods reviewed in the previous section.

1.4   Thesis outline

This dissertation comprises the description of a series of production and perception experiments investigating the issues outlined above. Chapters 3–6 have their own introductions and conclusions, having been written as independent articles. Therefore, there is an unavoidable degree of overlap between the introductory sections of these chapters, as well as with the general introduction. Chapter 2 provides a brief overview of the dialect situation in the Northern Isles, placed in its historical context. In Chapter 3, we will report on a production experiment investigating vowel and final consonant duration in monosyllabic words in Orkney and Shetland dialects, with Scottish Standard English and Norwegian as controls. The central aim of Chapters 4, 5 and 6 is to find experimental support for impressionistic claims that there are intonational differences between the dialects of Orkney and Shetland. Chapter 4 examines the role of intonation versus segmental information in the identification of Orkney and Shetland dialects by native listeners of each of these varieties. In Chapter 5, we will present the results of an acoustic investigation of the melodic and temporal differences between Orkney and Shetland dialects. Typical intonation contours, expressed in relative pitch-peak alignment and pitch level, were derived for the two dialects concerned. In the two listening experiments described in Chapter 6, the intonation contour has been systematically manipulated in order to establish the perceptual relevance of the prosodic parameters established in Chapter 5. Chapter 7 provides a summary of the work undertaken with an evaluation of the findings.

2   Orkney and Shetland: history and language

2.1   General

There is a striking difference between the landscapes of the two island groups. Shetland has a landscape very similar to that of the Scottish Highlands, with peat-covered hills and little arable land, while Orkney is flat, green and fertile. Westerly salt-laden winds and gales account for the general scarcity of trees in both Orkney and Shetland. Thanks to the Gulf Stream, the climate in the Northern Isles is relatively mild for its latitude.

Orkney lies just ten kilometres off the coast of northern Scotland and is inhabited by 19,245 people (2001 Census). The administrative centre is the town of Kirkwall, with a population of about 7,500. Agriculture, tourism and, since the 1970s, North Sea oil provide the main sources of income. Shetland is about 80 kilometres north-east of Orkney and has a population of 21,988 (2001 Census), some 7,500 of whom live in the capital, Lerwick.[6] Fisheries and North Sea oil and gas are key components of Shetland's economy, although in both Orkney and Shetland the importance of the oil industry has declined since the late 1990s.

2.2   History

The first inhabitants of Orkney and Shetland appear to have arrived during the Stone Age. Remains of their settlements, such as Skara Brae (Orkney) and Stanydale (Shetland), can still be found today. Archaeological evidence indicates that at the time of the first Viking raids, Pictish culture had become firmly rooted in both archipelagos.

Viking colonisers arrived in Orkney and Shetland in the first half of the ninth century, perhaps even earlier. Literary sources, such as the *Orkneyinga*

---

[6] Fair Isle (population 69), situated equidistant between Orkney and Shetland, belongs administratively to the latter.

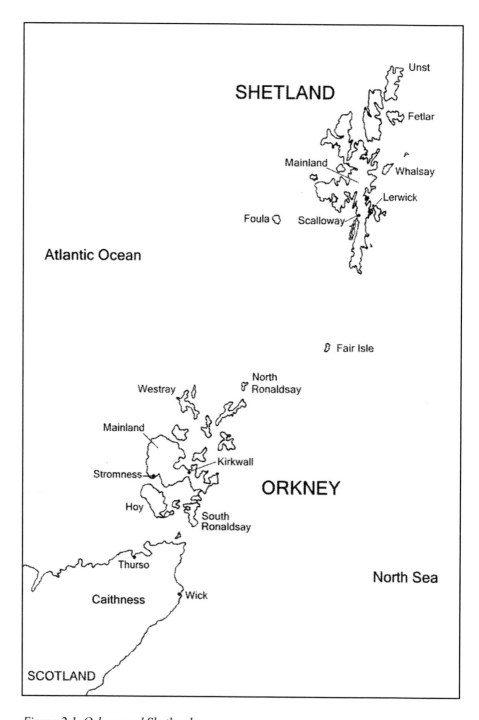

Figure 2.1. Orkney and Shetland.

Saga (the Icelandic account of the Orkney Earldom) suggest that the new settlers originated from south-west Norway. Place-name evidence from the Northern Isles seems to point to the same area (Stewart 1987). The Scandinavian language spoken by the immigrants and their descendants became known as 'Norrœna' (Northern language) or Norn, and it completely obliterated whatever languages were spoken by the Pictish inhabitants of the Isles. What happened to the indigenous people after the arrival of the Vikings is unclear, although it has been variously claimed that the natives were assimilated, driven out or exterminated (Barnes 1998, Smith 2001).

Powerful Norwegian *jarls* 'earls' ruled both island groups from their base in Orkney for several centuries. At its peak in the eleventh century, the Orkney Earldom extended from the Isle of Man in the south up to Shetland in the north, and included the Hebrides, Caithness and Sutherland.[7] The St Magnus Cathedral in Kirkwall was founded in 1137. However, Viking power began to wane at the end of the twelfth century and the earldom was split in 1195 when Shetland was forfeited to the Norwegian king after a power struggle (Crawford 2003). A few years later, the last Norse earl died without leaving an heir, and the earldom of Orkney passed to a Scottish family, although officially it remained Scandinavian territory. Scottish officials as well as people looking for new opportunities began to move into Orkney, taking their relatives, servants and friends with them. Meanwhile, Shetland maintained close relations with Norway and Shetland fish was sold through the Hanseatic *Kontor* in Bergen (Gade 1951).[8]

In 1468 Orkney and in 1469 Shetland were pledged to Scotland by King Christian I of Denmark and Norway, as security for his daughter's dowry on her marriage to the future James III of Scotland. The dowry itself was never paid, and this is how the islands became a Scottish province. By the time of the annexation, Orkney had become quite Scottish in character. After 1468, arable Orkney must be regarded increasingly as a remote part of feudal Scotland, rather than a mini-power in its own right. Oppressive Scottish landowners treated the grain-producing islands simply as a useful source of income (Thomson 2001). Life was not always easy in Orkney. In the seventeenth century, for example, the climate deterioration known as the 'Little Ice Age' shortened the growing season and great numbers of people

---

[7] Sutherland (ON *Suðrland* 'southern territory'), a (former) county in *northern* Scotland, takes its name from the perspective of the Orkney Earldom.
[8] Though not a member of the League, Bergen was a Hanseatic *Counter* 'privileged settlement'.

died in famines. Up until the present day, farming has constantly remained the mainstay of Orkney's economy.

In Shetland, developments took a somewhat different direction. After the transfer of the islands to Scotland, Scottish officials, and with them the Scots language, began to arrive in Shetland. At the same time, trade with northern Europe continued, and merchants from Hamburg and Bremen now sailed directly to Shetland for commercial purposes. The German ships arrived in April and returned home with dried herring at the end of August, a pattern that continued until well into the seventeenth century (Friedland 1983). Fishing has remained a dominant feature of Shetland's economy right up to the present day, even though many vessels are now being decommissioned and taken out of the fleet to reduce the number catching fish in order to preserve the rapidly dwindling stocks.

The distribution of surnames throughout the Northern Isles seems to reflect the diverging histories of Orkney and Shetland. The earliest recorded surnames in Scotland are those of Anglo-Norman families granted land by Scottish kings in the twelfth and thirteenth century. These names were generally taken from their estates in France or England and, later, Scotland. Imitating this trend, common people began to take surnames from local place-names from the fourteenth century onwards (Hough 2002). Orkney surnames are chiefly toponymic, and names like Linklater, Marwick and Isbister [aɪzbɪstər] all derive from place-names in Orkney. Shetland surnames were, just as in Scandinavia, typically patronymic, derived from the father's forename; hence, Sandy Johnson's son would be called Eric Sandison.[9] The patronymic names initially changed every generation, but in the course of the eighteenth century they became fixed (Beattie 2002).

Some Orkney surnames began to appear in Shetland after the 1500s, and this suggests that there was an influx of Orcadians following the annexation of Shetland by the Scottish Crown (Beattie 2002). Throughout the centuries, people continued to move to the Northern Isles (although many, of course, also left), and today we find many names originating from Central and North-East Scotland in both Orkney and Shetland. Nevertheless, even in 1990, toponymic names account for 43% of the 120 most common surnames in Orkney, against 33% in Shetland (but see above), and only 26% for Scotland as a whole. In Shetland, and in Scotland as a whole, relationship

_____

[9] Relationship names are also very common in mainland Scotland: *son* names in the Lowland area and *Mac* (the Gaelic word for 'son') in the Highlands.

names form the largest category (38% and 48%, respectively), while in Orkney just 28% of the surnames are of this type (Hough 2002).

2.3   Language

2.3.1 Life and death of Norn

There are scarcely any written records dating from the Scandinavian period in the Northern Isles; only some fifty runic inscriptions have been found in Orkney and seven in Shetland. The language of this small corpus appears to be west Scandinavian in character (Barnes 1993), although it is unclear whether the runes were carved by native islanders or visiting Norwegians (Barnes 1991). Furthermore, there are about a dozen extant Scandinavian-language documents in the Roman alphabet originating from Orkney and Shetland (Goudie 1904). Yet, the provenance of most of these documents is uncertain, and some of them could well have been written by Norwegians, possibly even in Norway itself (Smith 1996, Barnes 1998).

Literary references to the linguistic situation in the Northern Isles begin at the end of the sixteenth century; the principal sources are reprinted in Marwick (1929). What we can gather from these remarks, penned by ministers and visitors to the Isles, is that in the sixteenth century Norn seems to have been the language of the native population, although Scots was also well understood. Around the beginning of the eighteenth century, it appears that Norn as a first language was starting to lose ground rapidly. By the end of the century, Norn was referred to largely as a language of the past, even though some fragments of rhymes were still living on in the folk memory. The most remarkable feature in the documentary sources, as Smith (1996) points out, is that the writers never refer to any communication difficulties. This in striking contrast to the language problems faced by clergy working in Gaelic Scotland, and would suggest that bilingualism was general in the islands by the late sixteenth century.

In summary, it seems that Norn was spoken in the Northern Isles from its introduction by Viking settlers in the ninth century until its demise in the eighteenth century. After the annexation by Scotland, Lowland Scots became the language of administration, legislation, commerce and education. The process of the loss of the Norn language was clearly one of language shift (Barnes 1996). Occasions for speaking Norn outside the own family must have gradually decreased and, via an intermediate stage of bilingualism, the Northern Isles eventually abandoned Norn in favour of Lowland Scots.

In one sense, however, Norn has lived on until the present time (albeit imperfectly understood). The vast majority of place-names in the Northern Isles are of Norse origin (to give just two examples: *Kirkwall* < *Kirkjuvágr* 'kirk on the bay' and *Lerwick* < *Leirvík* 'mud bay').

Norn was never a literary language. Little is known about the development of spoken Norn in the centuries preceding its death since all we have are a few snatches of speech and verse and most Norn fragments were collected only *after* the language had gone out of everyday use. Most of these relics can be found in Jakobsen's (1928/1932) and Marwick's (1929) etymological dictionaries.[10] Jakobsen, a Faroese scholar, carried out his fieldwork trips to search out traces of Norn in the 1890s and the first decade of the twentieth century, and Marwick was an Orcadian inspired by Jakobsen. The picture that emerges from the surviving vocabulary collected by these scholars is that, in its final stages, Norn had been reduced to a language of the hearth.

2.3.2 Orkney and Shetland dialects today

Orkney and Shetland dialects are conservative varieties of Lowland Scots, with a substantial Norn substratum. It is notable that the vowel system of these dialects is still quite similar to that of Older Scots, and it is comparable to that of other peripheral Scots areas, such as Galloway in south-west Scotland. Scots was apparently taken to the Northern Isles by immigrants from Central Scotland in the sixteenth century at about the same time as it replaced Gaelic in Galloway (Catford 1957b). Furthermore, many Older Scots words that have been lost for some time in the Fife and Lothian area (cf. Grant and Murison 1931–1976) are still in everyday use in Orkney and Shetland, at least by the older generation.

It should also be noted that in Scots, we find many Scandinavian influences – both lexical and phonological – coming principally from the Anglo-Danish dialects of northern England. In the case of the Northern Isles, Scandinavian and Older Scots – two closely linked languages – were spoken side by side for several centuries, and many speakers were also bilingual. Therefore, it would be very difficult to distinguish direct Norn borrowings from indirect Scandinavian loans – a matter which we shall leave to historical linguists. In Lowland Scots, Scandinavian influences are

---

[10] According to Rendboe (1984, 1993), these Norn relics are in fact evidence that Norn was still spoken by some until well into the nineteenth century. This seems unlikely.

responsible for such phenomena as the absence of palatalisation in words as *kirk* 'church', *kist* 'chest' and *brig* 'bridge', the retention of [ʌu] in *nowt* — *check* 'cattle' and *grow* and lexical loans such as *big* 'build', *harns* 'brains' and *lug* 'ear' (McClure 1994). These features are also found in the dialects of the Northern Isles.

Within both Orkney and Shetland there is considerable regional diversity. Most of the islands constituting the archipelagos are quite small, and, for many centuries, there was little contact between them. Children went to school locally, and people generally married within their own parish. New trends, linguistic or otherwise, entered through the administrative centres, Kirkwall and Lerwick, and from there, spread slowly to the outlying areas. The glottal stop, for example, which has been a feature of Kirkwall and Lerwick speech for quite some time, seems to have arrived only recently in the rural areas. The dialect of the island of Whalsay differs considerably from all other Shetland varieties, and even native Shetlanders sometimes experience difficulty understanding this conservative variety. Nevertheless, in spite of the regional variation, it can safely be said that Orcadians speak Orkney dialect, and Shetlanders speak Shetland. As will be demonstrated in Chapter 4, a native of the Northern Isles seldom mistakes an Orcadian for a Shetlander, or vice versa; in Chapter 5, it will be shown why.

As for social varieties, there is no Scottish Standard English speaking middle class and virtually all native speakers, from manual workers to university graduates, employ the local dialect in their everyday speech. In fact, using a standardised form of English with locals, called *chanting* in Orcadian and *knapping* [kn] in Shetland, is much frowned upon (Melchers 1985). Orcadians and Shetlanders take a pride in the Norse heritage that sets them apart from mainland Scotland, and speaking the dialect is regarded as a way to emphasise this difference.

Since the late 1970s, however, the linguistic situation in the Northern Isles has started to change. Many people have moved from the outer isles into the towns of Kirkwall and Lerwick. Furthermore, there has been a wave of immigration from mainland Scotland and England into the Northern Isles, while at the same time young people born in the Isles increasingly remain in Edinburgh or Aberdeen after graduating from university. Until the 1960s, the percentage of people born outside Orkney or Shetland remained stable at around 10%. These incomers, or at least their offspring, generally acquired the local dialect. Yet, from the 2001 Census it can be deduced that an estimated 25 to 30 per cent of the people now living in the Northern Isles are

incomers, about half of them from England.[11] This situation has led to an
unprecedented levelling of the local varieties, and it appears that among
school children and teenagers a type of Standard English – rather than the
local dialect, or even Scots – is rapidly becoming the norm.

Finally, a few words need to be said about Caithness in the extreme
north-east of mainland Scotland.[12] During the Viking era, Caithness was part
of the Earldom of Orkney. Place-name evidence suggests that Scandinavian
influence there was confined chiefly to the coastal region (Waugh 1989).
Viking power in the area was relatively short-lived, and from the twelfth
century onwards Caithness became increasingly involved with Gaelic
Scotland. Linguistically, Caithness has long been a crossroads, with Gaelic
spoken in the south and west and Lowland Scots supplanting Norn in the
coastal areas. Throughout the centuries, features of Gaelic speech have crept
into Lowland Caithness speech (and vice versa). Even though present-day
Caithness dialect shares a number of characteristics with Orkney and even
Shetland dialect, Caithness speech is easily identified because of its highly
distinctive retroflex /r/, which is often also labialised (Mather 1978).[13, 14]

2.3.3   Features of Orkney and Shetland dialects

There exists no comprehensive account of twentieth-century Orkney and
Shetland dialects. Most references in the literature to aspects of these varieties
are based on sources such as the Linguistic Survey of Scotland (published in
Mather and Speitel 1975, 1977, 1986). However, this survey was carried out
largely in the 1950s, using predominantly elderly, rural informants; speakers
from the towns of Kirkwall and Lerwick were not included. Consequently,
the pronunciation features of Orkney and Shetland dialects as described by,
for example, Johnston (1997) are somewhat out of date.

---

[11] Note that the 2001 Census does not list separately the number of persons resident
in Orkney and Shetland who had actually been born there. However, in 1971
approximately 87% of islanders had been born locally, while 8% had been born in
mainland Scotland and 2% in England. By 2001, the percentage of English-born
residents had risen to 14% for Orkney and 11% for Shetland. Assuming a similar
rate of increase over this period for those born in mainland Scotland, one would
arrive at a figure for this group of around 15%.

[12] The county of Caithness became part of the Highland region in 1975.

[13] Caithness dialect is sometimes referred to as 'the third Norn dialect' (Thorsen
1954).

[14] Because of the retroflex /r/, and also because of their distinctive intonation,
Caithness speakers are often mistaken for Northern Irish.

A detailed description of present-day Orkney and Shetland dialects falls outside the scope of the present investigation. As mentioned in Chapter 1, the two dialects at issue seem to differ prosodically; this matter is the subject of the present investigation and will be discussed in the following chapters. What follows is a brief survey of some of the general characteristics of the local vernaculars, some of which might be attributed to Norn. Only features that I have been able to attest myself during recent fieldwork trips will be mentioned; the list does not aim to be exhaustive.

Lexis

Some Norn loan words found in Orkney and Shetland dialects are: *andoo* 'row a boat against the wind or tide' (ON *andefa*); *arvi* (Sh) or *arvo* (O) 'chickweed' (ON *arfi*); *piltock* 'young coalfish' (diminutive of ON *pilt* 'young boy'); *shalder* 'oystercatcher' (ON *tjalder*) and *skoit* (Sh) 'to look with a purpose' (cf. Dan. *skott*, Norw. dial. *skyttra*). The word *peedie* (O) or *peerie* (Sh) 'little' or 'small' (often employed as a kind of positive shibboleth to emphasise Orkney or Shetland loyalty) is of uncertain origin and has also been attested in nineteenth century Lothian and Fife speech (Grant and Murison 1931–1976).

Grammar and morphology

A friend, or someone younger, is addressed with familiar, friendly *du* (T); respectful *you* (V) is used to parents, older people or strangers. The T/V pronoun system is still in common use in Shetland, whereas in Orkney it seems to be dying out, and is now only found among elderly people in Westray.[15] (Note that *du* is second person singular, hence, *du sees*? 'you see?') Gender-marked pronouns are used for weather and time, for example, *He lowsed wi da rain* (Sh) 'It begins to rain heavily'. In Orkney, this usage seems to be on the way out.

The auxiliary *be* rather than *have* is used to form the perfect tense as in *I'm seen him* and *I'm bought* [bʌut] *biscuits*. The origin of this construction of *be* with transitive verbs is unclear. Owing to the lack of written evidence, we do not know whether this feature also occurred in Norn. Yet, since the construction is also found in Central Scotland (Trudgill and Hannah 1982), it might have been introduced to Orkney and Shetland by immigrants from this area (Melchers 1992, Pavlenko 1997). The Older Scots distinction of present

---

[15] Note that the T/V pronoun system is by no means unique to the Northern Isles; until recently it was also found in mainland Scotland as well as in England and Wales (cf. Wales to appear).

participle –*an* and verbal noun –*in* is maintained in both Orkney and Shetland, e.g. *I'm doan me cleanin*. We also find this feature in other peripheral Lowland Scots dialects, such as Caithness and Dumfriesshire. As in Scots, some of the verbs that have remained strong in Standard English have become weak, like *catch* – *catched* and *creep* – *creepit*. Some archaic irregular past tenses, like *wrought* [rʌut] 'worked', are used as well, albeit chiefly in the outlying areas.

Pronunciation

Orkney and Shetland dialects both preserve what are, in essence, systemically identical conservative Scots vowel inventories, even though lexical incidence is often radically different from mainland Scots dialects, and even varies considerably within the islands themselves. For example, in words like *find* [ɪ], *take* [a], *meat* [e] 'food' and *good* [ø] the Older Scots vowels have been retained, while in other cases vowels might be raised, diphthongised or fronted, as in *table* [i], *red* [i], *fish* [ɛi] and *part* [ɛ]. The vowel /ø/ also occurs in Norn loans as *buil* (Sh) 'resting place for animals, nest', *böd* (Sh) 'a small house in which fishing tackle is kept', as well as in place-names, for example, *Ouse* (a small bay in Shapinsay, Orkney).

Although the vowels are certainly of considerable interest, the main evidence of Norn substratal influences are probably to be discovered in the consonants of the islands. The use of [d] and [t] for /ð/ and /θ/, for example, *den* 'then', *tree* 'three' and *eart* 'earth', is generally thought to be due to the loss of these fricatives in Norn (Barnes 1998).[16] This so-called TH stopping (Wells 1982) is still a general feature of Shetland speech, but has largely been reversed in Orkney, and the feature is now only heard in the speech of elderly, rural natives. In fact, TH stopping seems to be creeping into the Standard English spoken by Shetland-born teenagers with English or mainland Scots parents (Cluness 2000, Scobbie to appear).

In both Orkney and Shetland dialects, the stops /p t k/ are voiceless unaspirated (cf. Chapter 3, footnote 19), while /b d g/ are fully voiced; there is, unlike Icelandic, Faroese and a few other Scandinavian varieties (cf. Helgason 2002, 2003) and, interestingly, Gaelic, no pre-aspiration of these stops. The voiced affricate /dʒ/ is typically devoiced to [tʃ], hence, *jar* and *just* become [tʃar] and [tʃʌst]; the occurrence of this devoicing decreases in more formal speech.

---

[16] See Chapter 3 for a discussion of the effect of the Scottish Vowel Length Rule of /d/ derived from historical /ð/ versus 'normal' /d/ in Shetland dialect.

It is worth noting that with respect to consonant realisation there seem to be dissimilarities between the two island groups, with Shetland pronunciation retaining a number of features that might be attributable to a Scandinavian substratum, while Orkney dialect seems to have lost many of these features. In conservative Shetland speech, for example, the initial consonant cluster /kn/ is retained, e.g. *knee* and *knowe* [knʌu] 'small hill' and, furthermore, initial /k/ and /g/ are palatalised, as in *kemp* [kjɛmp] 'to fight' and *geo* [gjo:] 'sea inlet'. In most varieties of Shetland speech, we also find palatalisation of post-vocalic alveolar consonants. As is typically the case with palatal consonants, this has the effect of raising the preceding vowel, and producing a palatal offglide, giving a diphthongal impression as can be heard in a local 'catch phrase' frequently employed to illustrate dialect features *ten men in the bed* [tɛ'n̩ mɛ'n̩ ɪn̩ də bɛ'd̩] and also in *later on* [o'n]. The feature is particularly noticeable in the pronunciation of speakers from Burra Isle (south-west Shetland) and is somewhat stigmatised. According to Catford (1957a), palatalisation of this type is not reported in mainland Scotland, but is, on the other hand, found in certain Norwegian dialects.

A further difference between the two varieties is heard in the typical realisations of /l/, with Shetland speakers producing word-initial /l/ with strikingly darker realisations than those found in Orkney speech. In intervocalic and final position, Shetland /l/ tends to vary, with some speakers having dark [l] in all contexts, while Orkney /l/ is generally clear [l] in these positions (note that clear /l/ is also a feature of Highland English and Gaelic). In both Orkney and Shetland, /l/ is often dropped in certain words with open back vowels, for example in *ba'* 'ball' [ba:], *fa'* 'fall' [fa:] and *wa'* 'wall' [wa:].

Finally, in Orkney speech, especially on Mainland (the largest of the Orkney Isles), word-final <–rse> is generally realised as [ɹʃ] as in, for example, *worse* [wʌɹʃ], *horse* [hɔɹʃ] and *nurse* [nʌɹʃ]; this feature seems to be unaffected by age or stylistic variation (Norquay 2003). This pronunciation is not found in Shetland; it does, however, occur in some varieties of Caithness speech.

2.4   Summary

The islands of Orkney and Shetland were colonised by Vikings from Norway in the ninth century. The Scandinavian language spoken by the settlers became known as Norn and remained the native language in the Northern Isles until the eighteenth century, when it was abandoned in favour of Lowland Scots. The histories of the two island groups diverged at an early stage. Fertile Orkney became involved with Scotland well before the islands were handed over to the Scottish King in 1468–9, while Shetland continued to look to Norway, and later also to north-west Germany, for its fish-trade. The conservative varieties of Lowland Scots presently spoken in Orkney and Shetland still have certain features that can most likely be ascribed to the Norn substratum.

3	The relationship between vowel and consonant duration in Orkney and Shetland dialects

In Shetland dialect, the northernmost branch of Lowland Scots, stressed monosyllables, when closed by a consonant, generally contain either a durationally short vowel followed by a durationally long consonant, or a long vowel followed by a short consonant.[17] This feature, first described in the 1950s, can most likely be ascribed to the Scandinavian substratum of the dialect. Although several experimental investigations into the duration of Scottish vowels have been carried out recently, most of them in the light of the Scottish Vowel Length Rule, none of them so far have looked at Shetland dialect or the relationship between the duration of the vowel and the final consonant. In this chapter, we will examine vowel and final consonant duration in monosyllabic words in both Shetland and Orkney dialects, as well as in Scottish Standard English and Standard Norwegian, in order to establish whether in Shetland dialect, durationally short consonants follow durationally long vowels and vice versa and if so, if this is indeed a feature peculiar to Shetland.

3.1　Introduction

According to Catford (1957a), one of the most general characteristics of Shetland dialect ascribed to the Norn substratum can be seen in the structure of the syllable.

> The essential feature of this is that stressed monosyllables, when closed by a consonant, generally contain either a short vowel (V) followed by a long consonant (CC), or a long vowel (VV) followed by a short consonant (C), e.g., type CVCC: 'baett'– beat, 'mett'– met, 'fatt'– fat, 'badd'– bad, 'henn'– hen, 'pott'– pot, etc., and type CVVC: 'bait', 'faat'– fault, 'fraad'– fraud, 'hain'– to economise, boat, etc. A somewhat similar phenomenon occurs in English and Scots generally, but the contrast between the two

---

[17] This chapter is a revision of van Leyden (2002).

types of syllable is much more clear-cut in Shetland than elsewhere, and associated with other peculiarly Shetland features. Since this type of syllable structure is a prominent feature of Norwegian, we feel justified in attributing it to Norn. (Catford 1957a:72)

In most Scandinavian dialects vowel length is not free, but can be predicted in stressed syllables. Vowels are long before short consonants and word finally, as in Norwegian *tak* [taːk] 'roof, ceiling'; elsewhere they are short, as in *takk* [tak:] 'thanks'. So, we find –V:C, –V:# and –VC: but not *–VC or *–V:C:. This system is the result of the Great Scandinavian Quantity Shift that took place between 1250 and 1550 (Haugen 1976).

In Lowland Scots and in Scottish Standard English (SSE) vowel length is not free either. The Scottish Vowel Length Rule (SVLR), which is the result of a sixteenth-century sound change, predicts that a stressed vowel, at least in a monosyllable, is phonetically short unless followed by a voiced fricative or /r/, in which case it is long. The vowel is also long if followed by a word or morpheme boundary, as in *agree#d* /iː/ versus *need* /i/. The SVLR does not apply to reflexes of Older Scots /ɪ/ and /ʊ/, i.e. Modern Scots /ɪ/ and /ʌ/, which are invariably short (Aitken 1981). However, recent experimental studies have revealed that the SVLR in working class and middle class Scottish Standard English applies only to the three vowels /i/, /u/ and /ai/ (McClure 1977, Agutter 1987, McKenna 1988). There appears to be as yet no published instrumental work focussing on the SVLR in rural Lowland Scots.

According to Árnason (1980:90–91) the most important difference between the SVLR and the Great Scandinavian Quantity Shift is that the main effect of the change in Scots has been a general shortening of long vowels, whereas the Scandinavian shift seems to have resulted in greater harmonisation of syllabic quantity. The importance one assigns to this difference depends on the criteria used. A typology based on the presence versus absence of free phonological length in vowels would put Scots in the same category as the Nordic languages, whereas a typology based on presence versus absence of fixed syllabic quantity would put Scots in the same category as English.

Returning to the dialect situation in the Northern Isles, Aitken (1981) points out that some apparent vowel length irregularities with contrastive effects do occur in Shetland dialect. In this variety, SVLR vowels before /d/ appear both with long and short realisations: as, [nidd] *need*, but [miːd] *meid* 'meith, landmark', and [gødd] *good* but [bøːd] *böd* 'fishermen's booth'. The items with the long realisations all derive from earlier forms with the voiced fricative /ð/ as the syllable closing consonant, i.e. one of the SVLR-long environments. Hence, once we know the etymology of a particular word we are able to predict the vowel duration.

Melchers (1984) analyses recordings made during her own fieldwork in addition to data collected in the Linguistic Survey of Scotland (published in Mather and Speitel 1975, 1977, 1986). She finds that vowel and consonant duration in monosyllables seem to follow the 'Scandinavian' pattern, but that the occurrence of long consonants tends to be restricted chiefly to Norn loanwords. Unfortunately, she does not give measurements to support her argument; nor does she provide the context in which the words were pronounced. Therefore, it is somewhat difficult to draw any conclusions regarding the syllable structure of Shetland dialect, or to compare her findings to other studies.

The aim of this chapter, therefore, is:

1. To establish whether in present-day Shetland dialect there are indeed both durationally long and short vowels as well as durationally long and short consonants in complementary distribution; and if so,
2. If we find a –V:C versus –VC: rhyme pattern throughout the Shetland vocabulary, or
3. If it is lexical-incidental and limited to word (pairs) of Norn origin and/or to words like *meid* 'landmark' and *böd* 'fishermen's booth', where the /d/ derives from historic /ð/, hence, words which are subject to the SVLR.

Furthermore, we will examine Orkney dialect and compare the Northern Isles' data with those of SSE, both with respect to vowel and final consonant duration as well as in the light of the SVLR. To address the questions outlined above, we carried out identical production experiments with speakers in Shetland, Orkney and Edinburgh.

3.2 Method

3.2.1 Materials

A total of 107 monosyllabic words was selected for the production experiment. With a few exceptions, the same words were used in all three geographic locations. The selection of the words was based both on the literature dealing with Shetland dialect (Catford 1957a, Aitken 1981) as well as on data gathered during recent fieldwork carried out by the author. Furthermore, providing they fitted our criteria, we tried to include the same words that were used in other studies investigating vowel duration in Scots (McClure 1977, Agutter 1987).

Our basic criteria in the selection of the materials were to include (1) a range of words that have a word-final /d/ derived from historical /ð/, i.e. a diachronic SVLR environment (Aitken 1981), together with (2) all word pairs cited by Catford (1957a). Additionally, we included a few sets of words claimed to be pairs by local informants.

In order to investigate the general effect of the vowel on the duration of the word-final consonant, we selected three final consonants: /r/, which provides a context designated lengthening by the SVLR, together with /t/ and /m/, which both provide a non-lengthening context. These consonants were examined in eighteen vowel contexts, including seven front vowels, six back vowels and four diphthongs. (Not all of the 54 theoretical possibilities (18 vowels * 3 final consonants) could be explored because of phonological constraints or 'gaps' in the lexicon.) We arrived at these categories on the postulate that the vowel categories distinguished in Older Scots largely correspond with those found in present-day conservative Shetland and Orkney dialects (Catford 1957b, Mather and Speitel 1975, 1977 1986, Johnston 1997).[18] Furthermore, we included one CV word for twelve of the eighteen vowel categories (lax vowels cannot occur in word-final position). A word boundary constitutes a SVLR environment and, therefore, we should expect to find only long realisations of the vowels in this context.

To examine the effect of the word-final consonant on the preceding vowel, two vowels were selected from the set of eighteen, namely /ɪ/, which is not affected by the SVLR and is therefore always short in duration, and /i/, which is reported to undergo the SVLR in Scots (Aitken 1981, Agutter 1987, McKenna 1988). For each of the vowels studied, the ancestral vowel in Older Scots was the same for all the monosyllables that were selected. Where there was no such word available, a substitute was found with synchronic /ɪ/ or /i/. The two vowels were examined in all possible consonant contexts and included six that are designated as lengthening by the SVLR (– #, – #d, – r, – v, – ð, – z), and fifteen that are designated non-lengthening (stops, nasals, etc.). The selected monosyllables are listed in Appendix 1.

It was assumed that vowel duration is not affected by the preceding consonant (Peterson and Lehiste 1960, Lindblom et al. 1981). Nevertheless, whenever possible, words beginning with a plosive, preferably voiced

---

[18] Aitken (1981) distinguishes 20 vowel categories for Middle Scots. However, it was decided not to investigate the reflexes of /ui/ and /ei#/, respectively /əi/ (as in *oil*) and /i/ (as in *dee* 'die') in Modern Scots.

(voiceless stops tend to be affricated in Shetland dialect), were used in order to achieve uniformity, as well as to facilitate the measuring task. Where no such words were available, we resorted to monosyllables with an initial voiceless fricative or a nasal. Failing those alternatives, we opted for words with an initial consonant of a different kind.

3.2.2 Subjects

The subjects comprised thirteen natives of Shetland, six male and seven female and between 30 and 50 years of age, twelve natives of Orkney, six male and six female of the same age group, and twelve native speakers of SSE (students of Edinburgh University, with an mean age of 25). The Shetland and Orkney informants had resided locally for most of their lives and used the local dialect on an everyday basis. In order to provide an overall view of the relationship between vowel duration and final consonant duration in the dialects, the informants were chosen from several parishes throughout the islands. The subjects participated on a voluntary basis and were not paid. None of the informants knew the purpose of the study until they were debriefed at the end of the experimental session.

3.2.3 Procedure

The selected monosyllables were read in a short fixed carrier phrase: *I say* [*word*] *again*. A fixed carrier phrase was used to control for intonation and reading speed. The stimuli were randomised and presented on four sheets of paper; the first and the last stimulus on each sheet served as fillers and were not analysed. Subjects were instructed to read at a natural speaking rate and to pronounce the sentences with a pitch accent on the target word. Prior to the recording session, subjects were given ample time to read through the material and they were also asked to indicate the meaning of the words. Each speaker recorded the list of materials twice, with a short break between the lists. The Shetland and Orkney speakers were individually recorded onto minidisc (Sony MZ–R35) in their own home or workplace; the Edinburgh speakers were recorded in a sound-insulated booth. The analogue output of the minidisc recordings was AD converted (16 kHz, 16 bit) and stored on computer disk for later analysis.

3.3   Results

3.3.1 Measurements

The data set nominally comprised in total 7,918 recorded utterances: 37 (speakers) * 107 (stimuli) * 2 (repetitions) for Shetland, Orkney and

Edinburgh. However, for each of the subjects, in order to keep the measuring task manageable, only the second recording of the material was analysed. Yet, in order to be able to decide whether the informants were linguistically reliable, the vowel and final consonant durations of ten randomly selected words from the first recording were measured for each of the subjects. The measured durations for a particular subject were then compared to segment durations of his or her second recording of the same words. Using the criterion that the vowel and final consonant durations of the second recording should not deviate by more than ±5% from the corresponding durations of the first recording, three subjects from Shetland, two from Orkney and two from Edinburgh were excluded from the experiment. Also excluded from the analysis were those cases where a speaker apparently did not know a particular word. These cases comprised 31 instances throughout the data set as well as 30 (3 words * 10 speakers) cases for Orkney and 50 (5 words * 10 speakers) for Edinburgh where none of the speakers was familiar with one particular word. Thus, the actual data set comprised [30 (speakers) * 107 (stimuli)] − 111 (unfamiliar words) = 3,099 tokens.

Segment durations of the target words were measured using a high-resolution waveform analyser (PRAAT software; Boersma and Weenink 1996) under both visual and auditory control. The utmost care was taken to apply the same segmentation criteria throughout the data set. Aspiration was considered to be part of the vowel and included in the total vowel duration (Klatt 1974).[19]

3.3.2 Analysis

3.3.2.1 Shetland

Mean segment durations for 93 (C)VC monosyllables were calculated across all ten Shetland subjects. (The 107 stimuli comprise 95 (C)VC words and 12 CV words. However, the words *pitch* and *beech* were excluded from the overall analysis because of the disproportional long duration, over 250 ms, of the /tʃ/.) Figure 3.1 represents the relationship between vowel (V) and final consonant (C^f) duration for (C)VC words in Shetland dialect.

---

[19] In most Lowland Scots dialects, initial voiceless stops have relatively little aspiration. In this study, the mean VOT for initial /p/ in Shetland dialect was found to be 22 ms (10 speakers, 9 words), whereas Orkney and Edinburgh speakers had a VOT of, respectively, 40 and 61 ms. However, the effect of these differences in VOT on the overall results appeared to be negligible.

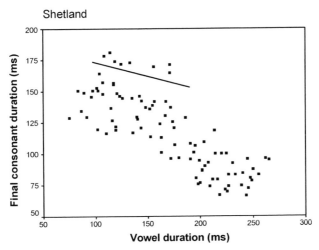

Figure 3.1. Relationship between vowel and final consonant duration for 93 (C)VC words in Shetland dialect. Data points represent test words; mean data of 10 subjects. (r = −0.799) The data points located above the line represent (C)VC words ending in a voiceless fricative.

As can be seen in Figure 3.1, there is a clear negative correlation between V and C^f duration: the longer the vowel, the shorter the final consonant. The product-moment correlation between V and C^f duration for the 93 measured (C)VC words is −0.799 (p < 0.01). The observed variation in V duration accounts for 64% ($r^2 = 0.638$) of the observed variation in C^f duration.

The relationship between V and C^f duration was further examined through simple linear regression analysis. Table 3.1 specifies the a (intercept) and b (slope) for the regression function predicting C^f duration from the corresponding V duration in Shetland dialect. The adequacy of the regression function is expressed by the correlation coefficient r, or better still, by the coefficient of determination r^2 (i.e. the percentage of the variance in C^f duration explained by V duration).

Table 3.1. a (intercept) and b (slope) for the regression function predicting C^f duration from the corresponding V duration in Shetland dialect ($C^f = V*b+a$). Correlation (r) and determination coefficients (r^2) are indicated. Mean data of 10 subjects.

	b	a	r	r^2
All data	−0.491	201	−0.799	0.638
−d	−0.612	208	−0.939	0.882
−t	−0.382	183	−0.836	0.698
−m	−0.470	210	−0.899	0.808

The results bear out that there is a considerable degree of compensation in the C^f duration, making up for changes in V duration. A 100 ms change in V duration is reflected by an inverse change in C duration of 49 ms. For the specific groups, the correlation coefficient is somewhat higher than for all test words together, while the b coefficients are within the same range. The compensatory mechanism is clearly stronger in the –d context, which is explained by the fact that the words ending in /d/ derived from historical /ð/ fall into this category; we shall return to these words below.

Figure 3.2 represents the relationship between vowel and final consonant duration for the five (semi-) minimal pairs (CV:C versus CVC:) as observed by Catford (1957a) (henceforth 'Catford pairs'). (Actually, Catford (1957a) listed eleven words. However, for some unspecified reason, a CV:C counterpart of *met* was not given.) These pairs are: *pot – boat, beat – bait, hen – hain* 'to economise', *fat – faut* 'fault' and *bad – fraud*.

The scattergram reveals that for the Catford pairs the relationship between vowel and final consonant duration is linear and that the CV:C member of a particular pair is located immediately below and to the right of its CVC: counterpart. The product-moment correlation between V duration and C^f duration for the Catford pairs is –0.903 (p < 0.01) and the b-coefficient with C^f duration as the dependent is –0.526. The variation in V duration accounts for 82% of the observed variation in C^f duration.

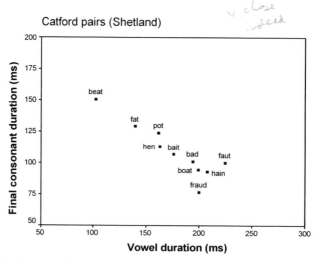

Figure 3.2. Relationship between vowel and final consonant duration for the Catford pairs (CV:C versus CVC:) in Shetland dialect. Mean data of 10 subjects. (r = –0.903)

The relationship between vowel and final consonant duration for a diverse set of words, including six pairs (CVC: versus CV:C) is represented in Figure 3.3. These pairs include: *clag* 'to clog' – *claag* 'to gossip, to chatter' (Sc. *claik*), *back* – *bauk* 'baulk, hen roost', *buil* 'resting place for animals' – *bruil* 'to bellow'. The remaining pairs (in Figure 3.3) consisted of a word with word-final /d/ derived from historical /ð/ (hence a diachronic SVLR environment; Aitken 1981) paired with a word including the same vowel, also ending in /d/, but derived from historical /d/: e.g. *bide* – *blide* 'happy', *deed* – *meid* 'landmark', *guid* 'good' – *böd* 'fishermen's booth'. In addition, we included *maed* 'maggot' and *saed* 'saithe', two words with word-final /d/ derived from historical /ð/ that could not be paired with a suitable word.

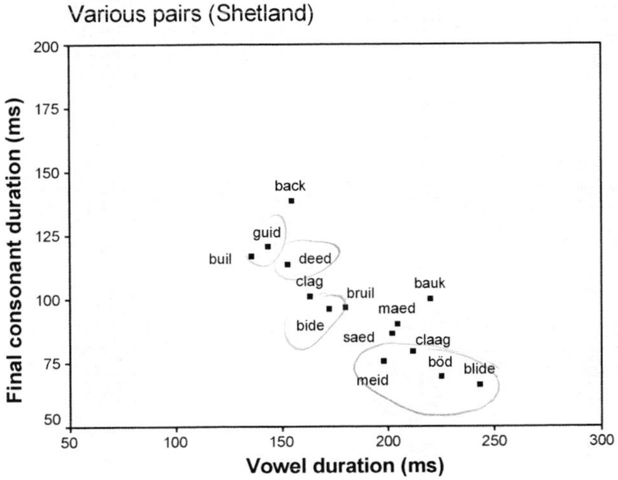

Figure 3.3. Relationship between vowel and final consonant duration for 14 words, including 6 pairs, in Shetland dialect. Mean data of 10 subjects. ($r = -0.849$)

Again, we can see that there is a clear negative correlation between vowel and final duration and that the CV:C member of a particular pair is located immediately below and to the right of its CVC: counterpart. The product-moment correlation between V and C^f duration for the fourteen words is -0.849 ($p < 0.01$) and the b coefficient with C^f duration as the dependent is -0.527. The variation in V duration accounts for 72% of the observed variation in C^f duration.

Closer examination of the measurements for the individual words reveals that the vowel duration of the three words ending in /d/, derived from historical /d/, is between 145 and 175 ms, whereas the vowel duration of the five words ending in /d/, but derived from historical /ð/ is between about 200 and 250 ms. Thus, the results reveal that the historical effect of the SVLR has indeed persisted up to the present day and they corroborate the vowel duration contrasts observed by Aitken (1981). We shall return to the effect of the SVLR on vowel duration in Section 3.5 below.

With respect to the vowels occurring in the pairs, it should be noted that the vowels of the Catford pairs, with the possible exception of the pair *hen – hain* (both words are pronounced as [hen]), not only differ in quantity but also in quality, whereas the vowels ([i], [ø] and [ai]) of the pairs which include a word with historical /ð/ as well as the pair *buil – bruil*, are spectrally identical. (Certain of the words examined may now have a different pronunciation from that used at the time of Catford's (1957a) investigations.) In the case of the Catford pairs, then, the vowel duration contrast is explained by the nature of the vowels involved.[20] According to Aitken (1981), the vowels /e/, /ɔ/ and /a/, as in respectively, *bait*, *boat* and *faut* 'fault', are, in many dialects outside Central Scotland, durationally long. This applies not only to SVLR-long, but also to SVLR-short contexts. Shetland appears to be a dialect of this type: the present experiment revealed a mean vowel duration of 107 ms for *mate*, while *bait* has a mean vowel duration of 176 ms. The vowel duration contrast between *buil* and *bruil* is most likely a relic of the historical contrast between [brøl] 'bump' and [brø:l] '(to) bellow' given by Jakobsen (1928/1932). As all informants supplied '(to) bellow' as the meaning of *bruil*, it seems that only the second meaning has survived, and with it a vowel of relatively long duration.

3.3.2.2 Orkney

Figure 3.4 represents the relationship between vowel and final consonant duration for 90 (C)VC words in Orkney dialect. (The 107 stimuli comprise 95 (C)VC words and 12 CV words. However, none of the informants was familiar with *hain*, *buil* or *bruil*; the words *pitch* and *beech* were agian excluded from the overall analysis because of the disproportional long duration of the /tʃ/.)

Examining the results for Orkney, we observe that, when compared to the data for Shetland, the correlation between vowel and final consonant duration is less clear-cut. The product-moment correlation between vowel duration and final consonant duration for the 90 measured (C)VC words is −0.588 ($p < 0.01$). The observed variation in V duration accounts for 35% ($r^2 = 0.346$) of the observed variation in C^f duration.

---

[20] Note that open vowels (such as the [a] in *fraud* and *faut*) are inherently longer in duration than closed vowels (like the [e] or [i] in *beat*).

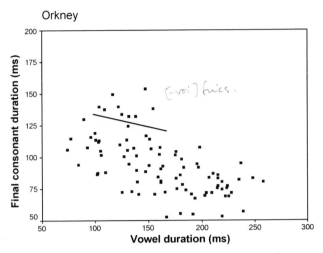

Figure 3.4. Relationship between vowel and final consonant duration for 90 (C)VC words in Orkney dialect. Data points represent test words; mean data of 10 subjects. (r = −0.588) The data points located above the line represent (C)VC words ending in a voiceless fricative.

Table 3.2 specifies the a (intercept) and b (slope) for the regression function predicting C^f duration from the corresponding V duration in Orkney dialect. The results show that, again, there is some degree of compensation in the C^f duration to make up for changes in V duration. In Orkney dialect, a 100 ms change in V duration is reflected by an inverse change in C duration of 29 ms. In other words, the compensatory mechanism is considerably weaker than is the case in Shetland dialect.

Table 3.2. a (intercept) and b (slope) for the regression function predicting C^f duration from the corresponding V duration in Orkney dialect. Mean data of 10 subjects. (Further see Table 3.1.)

	b	a	r	r^2
All data	−0.293	141	−0.588	0.346
−d	−0.210	99	−0.765	0.585
−t	−0.196	120	−0.671	0.450
−m	−0.264	140	−0.829	0.687

The relationship between vowel and final consonant duration for the Catford pairs and certain of the pairs listed in Section 3.3.2.1 above is represented in Figure 3.5, below. Unfortunately, it was not possible to examine exactly the same set of words as for Shetland; firstly, because of pronunciation differences; secondly, present-day Orkney speech has dental fricatives in words like *meid* or *saed*, and finally, Orkney speakers did not recognise the words *hain*, *buil* and *bruil*. The scattergram reveals that there appears to be little relationship between vowel and final consonant duration. The product-moment correlation between V and C^f duration for this particular selection of (C)VC words is -0.343 (p = 0.177); the observed variation in V duration accounts for 12% ($r^2 = 0.118$) of the observed variation in C^f duration; and the regression coefficient with C^f duration as the dependent variable is -0.168.

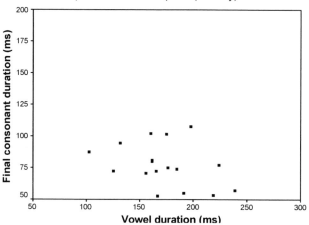

Various pairs and Catford pairs (Orkney)

Figure 3.5. Relationship between vowel and final consonant duration for 17 words, including the Catford pairs in Orkney dialect. Mean data of 10 subjects. (r = −0.343)

In Table 3.4 (in Section 3.3.2.3 below), we see that in Orkney dialect the vowel duration contrast between *mate* (short) and *bait* (relatively long) as observed in Shetland dialect is much less pronounced: the vowel duration of *bait* is only 14 ms longer than in the case of *mate*, while the difference in Shetland dialect is 69 ms for the same pair of words. The absence of this contrast, as well as of the short versus long contrasts between *pot* and *boat*, can most likely be ascribed to the fact that the influence of Central Scots dialects has, owing to its closer proximity to mainland Scotland, always been much stronger in Orkney than in Shetland.

3.3.2.3 Edinburgh

Figure 3.6 represents the relationship between vowel and final consonant duration for 92 (C)VC words in SSE. (The 107 stimuli comprise 96 (C)VC words and 11 CV words. However, none of the informants was familiar with

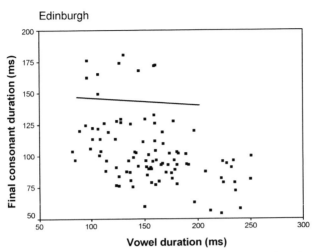

Figure 3.6. Relationship between vowel and final consonant duration for 92 (C)VC words in SSE. Data points represent test words; mean data of 10 subjects. (r = –0.443) The data points located above the line represent words ending in a voiceless fricative.

claik or *saithe*; the words *pitch* and *beech* were excluded from the overall analysis because of the disproportional long duration of the /tʃ/.)

Examination of the scattergram reveals that there is a weak, negative correlation between vowel and consonant duration. Note that the pattern of data points is similar to that in Figure 3.4 (above), which represents the results for Orkney. The product-moment correlation between V and C^f duration for the 92 measured (C)VC words is –0.450 (p < 0.01). The observed variation in V duration accounts for 20% (r^2 = 0.203) of the observed variation in C^f duration.

Table 3.3 specifies the a (intercept) and b (slope) for the regression function predicting C^f duration from the corresponding V duration in SSE. If we compare the regression coefficients for SSE to those for Orkney dialect in Table 3.2, we can see that they fall within the same range. In Edinburgh speech, therefore, a 100 ms change in V duration is reflected by an inverse change in C duration of 30 ms. The relationship between vowel and final consonant duration for the Catford pairs and the pairs listed in Section 3.3.2.1 above could not be examined, because of pronunciation and vocabulary differences between SSE and Orkney and Shetland dialects.

Table 3.3. a (intercept) and b (slope) for the regression function predicting C^f duration from the corresponding V duration in SSE. Mean data of 10 subjects. (Further see Table 3.1.)

	b	**a**	**r**	**r^2**
All data	−0.307	152	−0.450	0.203
−d	−0.229	106	−0.833	0.694
−t	−0.199	126	−0.751	0.564
−m	−0.302	162	−0.748	0.560

Table 3.4 presents the mean vowel duration in milliseconds broken down by word and geographic location. It appears that in SSE the difference in vowel duration between *mate* and *bait* (respectively, short versus relatively long in Shetland dialect) is, with 14 ms, the same as for Orkney dialect. When we compare the vowel durations of the pair *pot* and *boat* in either SSE or Orkney dialect with the vowel durations of the same words in Shetland dialect, we see a reverse contrast. *Pot*, in both SSE and Orkney dialect, has the longer duration of the two.

*Table 3.4. Vowel duration in ms broken down by word and geographic location. Mean data of 3*10 subjects.*

	mate	**bait**	**beat**	**pot**	**boat**
Shetland	107	176	103	162	199
Orkney	148	162	103	185	176
Edinburgh	144	158	100	161	142

3.4   Norway

In order to establish the relationship between vowel and final consonant duration in Scandinavian, a control experiment was carried out with speakers from Norway.[21] For this experiment, 50 Norwegian (C)VC words were

---

[21] Elert (1964) examined vowel and final consonant duration in Swedish, which also has a -V:C versus -VC: syllable structure. However, the findings of this study do not allow for a reliable comparison with our data as both mono- and polysyllabic words were examined in various context sentences. Additionally, the results were broken down by vowel and final consonant and expressed as a V/C ratio. We reanalysed a sample from the raw data in Elert (1964) (40 -VC words from a word list read by two speakers) and found that the regression slope coefficient with C^f duration as the dependent is −.490.

selected; the selected monosyllables are listed in Appendix 2. The words were read in a short fixed carrier phrase *Jeg sa* [*ord*] *alltid* 'I said [word] always' and digitally recorded by six native speakers of Bokmål Norwegian from the south-west coastal region of Norway. The Norwegian speakers were recorded in the *Norsk Sjømannskirke* 'Norwegian seamen's church' in Rotterdam. Segment durations of the target words were measured using the same criteria as for the other experiments.

The product-moment correlation between vowel and final consonant duration for the 50 measured Norwegian (C)VC words is –0.762. The regression function predicting C^f duration from V duration $C^f_i = (V_i*-0.570)$ + 269. Hence, a 100 ms change in V duration is reflected by an inverse change in C^f duration of 57 ms. When we compare this finding to the Scottish data, we see that in Shetland dialect a V duration increase of 100 ms results in a decrease of 49 ms in C^f duration, while the decrease in Orkney dialect and SSE is 29 and 30 ms, respectively.[22] Thus, the results indicate that the compensatory mechanism as found in Shetland dialect is almost as strong as in Norwegian.

3.5   The Scottish Vowel Length Rule in Orkney and Shetland dialects

As mentioned in Section 3.1 above, there appears to be as yet no published instrumental work focussing on the SVLR in rural Lowland Scots. Although the present experiment was primarily designed to investigate the relationship between vowel and final consonant duration, our selection of stimuli also allows a brief examination of the effect of the SVLR in Orkney and Shetland dialects as compared to SSE. Note, however, that of the about 350 theoretically possible (C)VC words only 107 have been explored and that these are distributed unevenly over the various categories; for example, we examined fourteen words ending in /r/, but only one with final /ð/.

Table 3.5 presents the mean vowel duration in milliseconds broken down by SVLR context and geographic location. It can be seen that, in SVLR-short contexts, the vowel duration of (C)VC words is about equal in all three locations, while in SVLR-long contexts in Shetland the mean vowel duration appears to be somewhat longer than in either Orkney or SSE. With respect to

---

[22] A small control experiment with 5 native Dutch speakers showed that a V duration increase of 100 ms results in a decrease of just 16 ms C^f duration. See Appendix 3 for further details.

words ending in /d/ deriving from historical /ð/ (i.e. a historical SVLR-long context), we see that the mean vowel duration of this particular set of words is almost within the same range as for the vowels in synchronic SVLR-long contexts.

Table 3.5. *Vowel duration in ms broken down by SVLR context and geographic location. Mean data of 3*10 subjects.*

	SVLR context			
	short	**voiced fric, −r, −#d, −#s**	**open syll.**	**−d (hist ð)**
Shetland	150	232	274	215
Orkney	148	208	252	187
Edinburgh	148	188	260	−

Examination of the mean vowel duration for the words *kite*, *bide*, *blide* and *blithe*, which are displayed in Table 3.6, reveals that in Shetland dialect the vowel duration of both *kite* and *bide* is relatively short when compared to *blide* (historical SVLR-long context).[23] Conversely, in Orkney and SSE, *bide* appears to have the longest vowel duration, while *blide* has a vowel duration within the same range as *kite*, or, in SSE in the case of *blithe*, is even about 40 ms shorter in duration than *kite*. (The Edinburgh informants pronounced *blithe* with a voiceless/devoiced 'th'.)

Table 3.6. *Vowel duration in ms broken down by word and geographic location. Mean data of 3*10 subjects.*

	kite	*bide*	*blide*	*blithe*
Shetland	176	172	243	−
Orkney	210	238	218	−
Edinburgh	207	212	−	177

As stated earlier, the main diachronic effect of the SVLR in Scots has been a general shortening of long vowels. In the case of Shetland dialect, therefore, the SVLR still applies today and conditions a relatively short vowel in both *kite* and *bide*. On the other hand, in Orkney dialect and SSE, the rule appears

---

[23] In Scottish English, duration is linked to quality in these diphthongs. In 'pie' (SVLR-long environment) the diphthong is more open [paˈe] than in 'kite' [kʌit] (SVLR-short environment).

not to operate in a similar way since the longest vowel duration is found in *bide*. The most likely explanation for this finding is that these dialects are being influenced by Standard English, a variety which has relatively long vowel durations preceding voiced as opposed to voiceless consonants (Gimson 1962).

3.6   Discussion and conclusion

Three identical production experiments were carried out with speakers in Shetland, Orkney, Edinburgh and Norway to examine vowel and consonant duration in monosyllabic words in order to establish whether in Shetland dialect, durationally short consonants follow durationally long vowels, and vice versa, and if so, if this is a feature peculiar to Shetland. Additionally, we looked briefly at the role of the SVLR.

It was found that, in Shetland dialect, vowel and final consonant duration are inversely related and, although this inverse relationship appears to be somewhat stronger for specific sets of local dialect words considered to constitute pairs, it appears that there is indeed a strong tendency towards a –V:C versus –VC: rhyme pattern throughout the vocabulary. In Orkney as well as in SSE a similar, but considerably weaker, relationship was found. As for vowel duration, the sets of words considered to constitute pairs in Shetland dialect appear not to behave similarly in either Orkney dialect or SSE. As for Norwegian, we found that the inverse relationship between vowel and final consonant duration was slightly stronger than for Shetland dialect. Therefore we conclude that, with respect to this prosodic characteristic, Shetland is not only geographically, but also linguistically, somewhat closer to Norway than to Central Scotland. In Orkney dialect, this particular relic of Norn has apparently been lost, most likely because of the strong influence of mainland Scots dialects.

The seeming vowel length irregularities with contrastive effects that are found in Shetland dialect can most likely be ascribed to historical developments involving the SVLR. For example, the vowels in *böd* 'fishermen's booth' and *meid* 'landmark' are long because they occur in a SVLR-long context, namely preceding historic /ð/. The vowel in *bait*, which derives from Older Scots /ai/, has remained long because this particular vowel is, at least in dialects outside Central Scotland, unaffected by the SVLR. In Central Scots dialects, the /e/ in *bait* has merged with the /e/ of *mate* (a reflex of Older Scots /aː/), a vowel which is shortened in SVLR-short contexts, and, as our data indicate, this merger has also taken place in Orkney dialect.

The social and economic situation in the Northern Isles has been changing rapidly since the advent of the oil boom in the early 1970s. As we saw in Chapter 2, more than 25% of the total population in both Orkney and Shetland are now of English or mainland Scottish origin (2001 Census). These incomers are predominantly families with young children, with the result that in some primary schools up to 50% of the pupils are of mainland Scottish or English origin and that SSE, or even Standard English, seems to have become the norm among the younger generation. Preliminary investigations indicate that in the speech of Shetlanders born after about 1970, the inverse relationship between vowel and final consonant duration is, indeed, weaker than in the speech of people who grew up before the oil boom. Therefore, it seems likely that this feature of the Norn substratum could be lost within a few generations.

4   Prosody versus segments in the identification of Orkney and Shetland dialects

This chapter examines the relative importance of intonation and segmental structure to the mutual identifiability of Orkney and Shetland dialects by native listeners of each of these varieties.[24] In both normal (intelligible) and LP-filtered (unintelligible) speech, three types of test utterance were generated: original intonation, monotonised speech, and transplanted melodies. In Experiment 1, listeners proved quite able to distinguish Orkney from Shetland speech on the basis of the intonation contour only. In Experiment 2, it was shown that the intonation contour was a more important cue than segmental information for Orkney but not for Shetland listeners. This result contradicts both earlier findings and common-sense reasoning, suggesting that prosodic differences are always secondary cues in the identification of language varieties.

4.1   Introduction

Shetland speech appears to have retained its Norn substratum to a greater degree than has Orkney. Dialect differences are apparent in the lexicon, the pronunciation and the syllable structure. However, the most striking difference between Orkney and Shetland speech is the dissimilarity in intonation. Impressionistically, Shetland dialect has a rather narrow pitch range, while Orkney speech has a relatively wide pitch range and is characterised by a distinctive, lilting, rise-fall intonation pattern whereby the pitch rise occurs relatively late in the word. According to popular belief, there are affinities in intonation between Orkney dialect and varieties of Norwegian and, indeed, rise delay has also been reported for a number of Scandinavian language varieties, such as Danish (Thorsen 1980) and Swedish (Bruce 1977). Still, it is somewhat unexpected that Orkney dialect

---

[24] A preliminary version of this chapter has appeared as van Leyden and van Heuven (2003).

should have 'Norwegian' intonation while, in other respects, Shetland dialect appears to be the more Scandinavian of the two varieties (cf. Chapter 3).

Native Shetlanders typically claim that it is very easy to identify an Orcadian by his intonation alone. Results of experiments investigating the role of intonation in the recognition of dialects indicate that intonation is, indeed, an important cue in the identification of regional varieties, particularly when identifying one's own dialect (Gooskens 1997, Gooskens to appear, Schaeffler and Summers 1999, Peters et al. 2003. Nevertheless, research – on English as well as on other languages – consistently shows that speech melody plays a *less* important role than segmental information in the identification of language varieties (Gooskens 1997, Gooskens and van Bezooijen 2002 and references therein). With a view to challenging this generalisation, we tested the importance of intonation versus segmental information to the identification of Orkney and Shetland dialects (with Standard Scottish English, SSE, as a control condition) by native listeners of each of these two varieties.

Two experiments will be discussed here. In Experiment 1, we explored to what extent native Orkney and Shetland listeners are able to distinguish between the two dialects. Using an experimental design similar to that of Gooskens and van Bezooijen (2002), we presented speech fragments both with and without the original intonation contour, in order to examine the contribution of prosody (more specifically, intonation) in the identification process. Although the elimination technique is suitable for demonstrating the role of intonation in distinguishing between dialects, it does not allow us to quantify the relative importance of intonation and segmental information in the perceptual identification of the language varieties. In Experiment 2, therefore, we examined the relative contribution of intonation and segmental information to the mutual identifiability of the target dialects by presenting speech both with and without the original melody, as well as speech fragments in which segmental and prosodic information were in conflict, i.e. by artificially exchanging the pitch curves between realizations of the same sentence in the two dialects while keeping the segmental information unaffected. Obviously, if an utterance spoken by a Shetlander (i.e. containing Shetland segmental information) but with an Orcadian intonation pattern is identified as produced by a speaker from Orkney, then intonation is the stronger of the two sets of cues. If, on the other hand, the listeners judge the hybrid utterance to be spoken by a Shetlander, then the segmental properties outweigh the intonational cues.

4.2 Experiment 1: The role of intonation

4.2.1 Method

4.2.1.1 Stimulus materials

The main aim of this experiment is to find experimental support for impressionistic claims that the dialects of Orkney and Shetland can be identified solely on the basis of prosodic information. Short fragments of spontaneous speech were presented to native listeners of the two dialects. The fragments were taken from brief, informal interviews recorded during earlier fieldwork trips. Six male speakers were selected; three from Orkney (West Mainland, Kirkwall and Westray) and three from Shetland (Burra Isle, West Mainland and North Mainland).[25] The sole selection criterion was that the selected speakers had to come from different parishes throughout Orkney and Shetland and had produced ample fluent speech during the interview; none of the speakers spoke very broad dialect. All speakers were between 35 and 50 years of age. The selected speech fragments were about twelve seconds in duration and comprised one or more syntactic sentences of semantically neutral content; only one fragment per speaker was included. Transcripts of the fragments are given in Appendix 4.

Two speech conditions were created: (1) normal (intelligible) speech and (2) LP-filtered (unintelligible) speech. LP-filtering delexicalises the speech signal by removing most of the spectral information while leaving the temporal organisation (intonation and syllable structure) intact. In this way, it is possible to investigate how well listeners are able to identify a language variety on the basis of prosody only. Using PRAAT speech processing software, the speech signal was LP-filtered at 300 Hz, with a band smoothing of 50 Hz. See Appendix 5 for an illustration of LP-filtered speech.

In both normal and filtered speech, two intonation conditions were generated: (1) original speech melody and (2) monotonised speech. By eliminating the intonation contour (through monotonisation), we are able to establish the importance of speech melody in distinguishing between the two dialects at issue. The condition with unintelligible, monotonous speech allows us to examine the role of temporal organisation and intensity in the

---

[25] Female speakers were not included, because applying the same low-pass filter for both male and female voices leaves relatively more traces of spectral information in the female speech. Hence, inclusion of both sexes could possibly introduce an additional variable that would have interfered with our results.

identification of Orkney and Shetland dialects.[26] Monotonisation was done with PRAAT software by changing the pitch contour into a flat line, using PSOLA analysis and resynthesis (Moulines and Verhelst 1995). This line was given no declination, since the distinguishing role of declination in Orkney and Shetland dialects is not known.

monotonis-ation

The manipulated speech fragments were converted from digital (16 KHz, 16 bit) to analog (allowing a signal bandwidth of just less than 8 KHz) and then recorded onto minidisc using a Sony MZ–R35 minidisc recorder and organised into four blocks, with fragments randomised within each block in the following way: (1) LP-filtered speech, monotonised; (2) LP-filtered speech, original intonation contour; (3) original speech, monotonised and (4) original speech, original intonation contour.

In order to compensate for a possible learning effect, two counter-balanced lists were created for each block. The interstimulus interval was four seconds (offset to onset); an alert tone was played one second prior to each stimulus onset.

4.2.1.2 Subjects

Twenty listeners took part in the experiment, ten from Orkney (six male and four female) and ten from Shetland (six male and four female). The subjects were chosen from several parishes throughout Orkney and Shetland and were between 30 and 50 years of age, having resided locally most of their lives. The listeners reported no hearing problems and were not paid for their participation.

4.2.1.3 Procedure

The subjects were tested individually in their own home or workplace in experimental sessions lasting about fifteen minutes including instruction time. The stimuli were presented over headphones (Sennheiser HD 455) at a comfortable listening level. Subjects were issued with response sheets on which they were asked to indicate, for each utterance, where they thought a particular speaker hailed from. They responded by ticking on a 10-point scale running between 1 'definitely from elsewhere' and 10 'definitely from Orkney' (for Orkney listeners) or 'definitely from Shetland' (for listeners in

---

[26] Note that Gooskens and van Bezooijen (2002) omitted this condition. Note also, that in previous studies (e.g. Cohen and 't Hart 1970), listeners were apparently unable to distinguish between language varieties when presented with unintelligible, monotonous speech.

Shetland). See Appendix 6 for a sample response sheet. Subjects were required always to tick a scale position, even if they felt they had to guess. It should be noted that, since the scale has no midpoint, the listeners were always forced to make a decision, no matter how tentative.

The four blocks of stimuli were played in the following order:

1. LP-filtered speech, monotonised
2. LP-filtered speech, original intonation contour
3. Original speech, monotonised
4. Original speech, original intonation contour.

That is, the presentation of material was so arranged that the amount of *[increasing amount of info]* linguistic information that was made available to the listeners increased from one block to the next, so as to prevent listeners from transferring information gathered from one block over to the next. Each block was preceded by two practice fragments, recorded by speakers other than those used in the experiment; responses to these trials were not included in the analysis.

4.3 Results

A total of 20 (subjects) * 6 (speakers) * 4 (presentation conditions) – 1 (missing response) = 479 responses were collected. The judgement scores were analysed by separate two-way analyses of variance (ANOVA) for intelligible and unintelligible speech, further broken down by listener group (Orkney and Shetland), assuming fixed factors for speech condition and dialect (Orkney or Shetland). Figure 4.1 presents the mean judgement scores broken down by presentation condition and by dialect. *[intonation contour doesn't contribute much]*

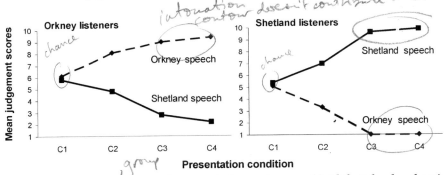

Figure 4.1. Spontaneous speech: mean judgement scores (1 'definitely elsewhere'; 10 'definitely my island'), broken down by presentation condition (C1–4) and by dialect, for Orkney listeners (left) and Shetland listeners (right). C1 = LP-filtered & monotonous; C2 = LP-filtered & original intonation contour; C3 = normal speech & monotonous; C4 = normal speech & original intonation contour. Mean data of 10 subjects per listener group.

As can be seen in Figure 4.1, for Orkney listeners, there is a large effect resulting from the dialect of the speaker, $F(1,231) = 313.8$ ($p < 0.001$), which strongly interacts with presentation condition, $F(3,231) = 42.8$ ($p < 0.001$), with judgement scores differentiating incrementally as a function of the linguistic cues that were made available to the listener. Similar, in fact, even larger, effects are observed for Shetland listeners, $F(1,232) = 919.7$ ($p < 0.001$) for the effect of speaker dialect and $F(3,232) = 134.3$ ($p < 0.001$) for the dialect * condition interaction.

Clearly, condition C1 (monotonous, unintelligible speech) contains no audible information that allows our listeners to differentiate between the two varieties. When the intonation contour is preserved in the unintelligible speech condition (C2), the origin of the speakers is distinguished rather well. However, when monotonised, *intelligible* speech is presented (C3), the differentiation between the varieties is nearly maximal. From this outcome it can be concluded that the two dialects differ distinctly with respect to their segmental structure. Finally, combining both information sources (C4) yields even better differentiation.

4.4   Experiment 2: Intonation versus segments

In experiment 1, the elimination technique proved suitable for demonstrating the role of intonation in distinguishing between dialects. However, the method is rough and ready. There is no direct comparison between segmental and prosodic cues. Even though we found that adding segmental information to condition C1 affords better identification of dialect than adding intonation, there is no guarantee that segmental information overrides intonation in a direct manner. Moreover, the elimination method does not control for a number of potential cues. For one thing, since segmental information is eliminated through LP-filtering, the differences in loudness between individual vowels due to concentration of energy in different parts of the spectrum are also eliminated. Moreover, low-pass filtering destroys crucial prosodic cues, such as syllable and word boundaries.

In Experiment 2, therefore, we examined the relative contribution of intonation and segmental information to the mutual identifiability of Orkney and Shetland dialects (with Scottish Standard English, SSE, as a control condition) by presenting speech both with and without the original melody, as well as speech fragments in which segmental and prosodic information were in conflict.

4.4.1 Method

It can be expected that spontaneous speech is most varied with respect to intonation (cf. Cruttenden 1997:128); however, for the investigation at hand, it was decided to use speech that was read aloud, rather than spontaneous speech, as it would have been too difficult to elicit suitable speech material during interviews.

4.4.1.2 Stimulus materials

Recordings of the utterance *There are many gardens in Bergen*, pronounced with a pitch accent on *gardens*, were selected from the corpus collected for the acoustic study in Chapter 5. Five male speakers were selected: Orkney 1 (ork1) and Orkney 2 (ork2) from Orkney (Kirkwall), Shetland 1 (sh1) and Shetland 2 (sh2) from Shetland (West Mainland) and one SSE speaker from Central Scotland. The main criteria in the selection of the speakers were matching voice quality as well as speaking rate. The Orkney and Shetland speakers were aged about forty; the SSE speaker was nineteen years of age.

Three speech conditions were generated: (1) LPC-resynthesised speech (intelligible), (2) 'buzz' (unintelligible) and (3) LP-filtered speech (unintelligible). As in Experiment 1, the speech signal was LP-filtered at 300 Hz, with a band smoothing of 50 Hz. However, not all spectral information is removed by LP-filtering and the remaining information might thus play a role in the identification process. Therefore, it was decided to use a second unintelligible 'speech' condition, which does not contain any spectral information. Using PRAAT software, a buzz was created by replacing segmental information by a spectrally invariant buzz-like sound (sawtooth wave) while preserving the amplitude and fundamental frequency modulations of the original, consequently, all spectral information was removed from the speech signal but prosodic variation was maintained. In this way, we could be certain that the perceptual identification of a particular language variety was based on prosodic cues only. LPC-resynthesis (autocorrelation method; Markel and Gray 1976) was carried out in order to conceal the identity of the speakers.[27] (In these small island communities,

---

[27] In LPC resynthesis as applied here, i.e. without adding the residual error signal to the output, the voice quality of the speaker is affected to some extent, as the excitation signal is no longer the speaker's original glottal pulse but an artificial sawtooth wave. Because of this substitution, LPC-resynthesised voices should resemble each other more than the originals. Still, speakers remain more or less identifiable since the resonance characteristics of the supraglottal tract (i.e. the formant structure) of the original speaker are maintained in the resynthesis.

there is a good chance that listeners personally know one or more of the speakers.) Speech was analysed and resynthesised with five formants and the associated bandwidths in the 0 to 5 kHz range, with a sawtooth wave as the source signal in the resynthesis; crucially, no residue (or error signal) was used in the resynthesis. The resulting quality was highly intelligible but – at least in the short utterances used for our experiment – masked the speaker's identity to some extent.[28] See Appendix 7 for spectrograms of LPC-resynthesised as well as buzzed speech.

For each of the three speech conditions (buzz, LP-filtered, LPC-resynthesised), three types of test utterance were generated:

1. Monotonous
2. Original intonation (stylised)
3. Transplanted melodies

Monotonisation was done by changing the pitch contour into a flat line; this line was given no declination (cf. Experiment 1). The utterances were monotonised at 100 Hz.

Stylised versions of the original intonation contours were made in order to afford easy exchange of melodies between segmentally similar utterances (condition 3 'transplanted melodies'). The stylisations were so-called close copies as defined within the IPO tradition of intonation research ('t Hart, Collier and Cohen 1990). A close copy is defined as 'a synthetic approximation of the natural course of pitch, meeting two criteria: it should be perceptually indistinguishable from the original, and it should contain the smallest possible number of straight-line segments with which this perceptual equally can be achieved' (Nooteboom 1997:646).[29]

The following transplantations were implemented: Orkney contours grafted onto the Shetland and the SSE utterances, Shetland contours superimposed on the Orkney and SSE utterances and SSE contour on the Orkney and the Shetland utterances. Furthermore, to make the design fully orthogonal, the contours of the two Orkney speakers (ork1 and ork2) were interchanged, as were the two Shetland contours (sh1 and sh2). For each original utterance, F0 was extracted (autocorrelation method) and interactively stylised, allowing at most one linear rise and one linear fall per syllable. The time coordinates of the pivot points in the resulting rise-fall

---

[28] Listeners were debriefed after their participation in the experiment. In no case could a participant identify any of the speakers they had heard on the tape.

[29] In the IPO tradition, the straight lines are defined in logarithmic plots (fundamental frequency in semitones) as a function of linear time.

sequence were expressed relative to the onset and offset of the syllable. The same relative timing of rises and falls was observed after transplantation of the contour; the frequency values of the transplanted contours were left as measured in the original environment. Table 4.1 gives an overview of the stimulus types; the five intonation contours are illustrated in Figures 4.2–6.

Table 4.1. Overview of stimulus types. See text for explanation of labels.

	Pitch contour					
Speaker	**ork1**	**ork2**	**sh1**	**sh1**	**SSE**	**monotonous**
ORK1	+	+	+	+	+	+
ORK2	+	+	+	+	+	+
SH1	+	+	+	+	+	+
SH2	+	+	+	+	+	+
SSE	+	+	+	+	+	+

The manipulated utterances were converted from digital (16 KHz, 16 bit) to analog (allowing a signal bandwidth of just less than 8 KHz) and then recorded onto minidisc using a Sony MZ–R35 minidisc recorder and organised into six blocks as follows: (1) buzz and monotonised; (2) buzz and (manipulated) intonation contour; (3) LP-filtered and monotonised; (4) LP-filtered and (manipulated) intonation contour; (5) LPC-resynthesised and monotonised; (6) LPC-resynthesised and (manipulated) intonation contour. The stimuli were randomised within each block. Two counterbalanced lists were created for each block, so as to cancel possible learning effects. The block of intelligible speech (LPC-resynthesised) was always presented last in order to prevent listeners from transferring information gathered from this ·block to the unintelligible blocks (buzz and LP-filtered). There were two presentation orders, as follows.

Sequence I Buzz and monotonised
Buzz and (manipulated) intonation contour
LP-filtered and monotonised
LP-filtered and (manipulated) intonation contour
LPC-resynthesised and monotonised
LPC-resynthesised and (manipulated) intonation contour

Sequence II LP-filtered and monotonised
LP-filtered and (manipulated) intonation contour
Buzz and monotonised
Buzz and (manipulated) intonation contour
LPC-resynthesised and monotonised
LPC-resynthesised and (manipulated) intonation contour

Because of the shortness of the stimuli (about 1.5 seconds), it was decided to make each test utterance audible twice successively, with an interval of one second separating the two tokens. The interstimulus interval was 3.5 seconds (offset of second token to the onset of the first token of the next stimulus); an alert tone was played one second prior to each stimulus onset. To summarise, each stimulus was presented as follows: beep – one second silence – stimulus – one second silence – (repetition of) stimulus – time for participant to write; beep – next stimulus.

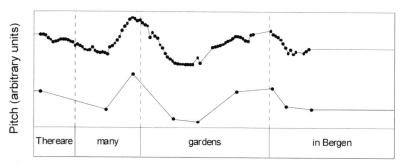

Figure 4.2. Original and stylised intonation contour of speaker Ork1 (with creaky voice in 'Bergen', hence no pitch points).

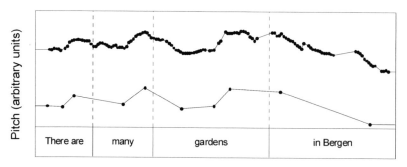

Figure 4.3. Original and stylised intonation contour of speaker Ork2.

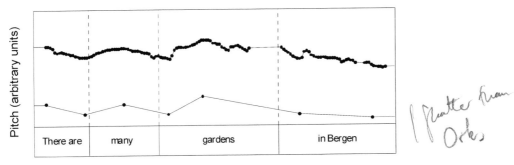

Figure 4.4. Original and stylised intonation contour of speaker Sh1.

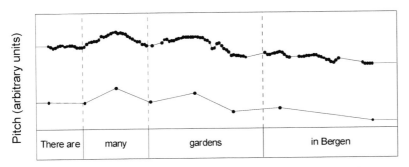

Figure 4.5. Original and stylised intonation contour of speaker Sh2.

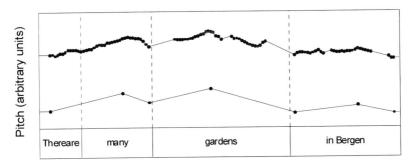

Figure 4.6. Original and stylised intonation contour of SSE speaker.

4.4.1.2 Subjects

Thirty-nine listeners took part in the experiment, nineteen from Orkney (ten male and nine female) and twenty from Shetland (ten male and ten female). The subjects were chosen from several parishes throughout Orkney and Shetland and were between 30 and 50 years of age, having resided locally for most of their lives. They reported no hearing problems and were not paid for their participation. Some of the listeners had also participated in Experiment 1. Ten Orcadians and ten Shetlanders listened to sequence I; nine Orcadians and ten Shetlanders listened to sequence II.

4.4.1.3 Procedure

The experimental procedure was identical to the procedure described in Section 4.2.1.3 above.

4.5   Results

The experiment yielded a total of 39 (subjects) * 30 (pitch manipulations) * 3 (speech conditions: buzz, LP-filtered and LPC-resynthesised) – 1 (missing response) = 3,509 responses. First, we will look at the responses for original intonation as well as monotonous speech. The role of segmental information (speaker dialect) versus intonation in the identification process will be dealt with in Section 4.5.2.

4.5.1   Spontaneous versus read speech

Experiment 1 revealed that native listeners distinguished quite clearly between Orkney and Shetland dialects when presented with *spontaneous* (informal) speech. For the present investigation, however, we used *read* (formal) speech. It has been demonstrated in numerous sociolinguistic studies that speakers use a more standardised variety of their language when reading than when speaking spontaneously (e.g. Labov 1972). According to Cruttenden (1997:128), it seems that there is also intonational variation between formal and informal speech. Yet, little is known about the effect of stylistic intonational variation on the perception of nativeness. Therefore, in order to establish how well listeners are able to distinguish between the dialects when presented with read speech, we extracted the responses for original intonation as well as monotonous speech (i.e. the same conditions as examined in our first experiment) from the data set.

The judgement scores were analysed by separate two-way analyses of variance (ANOVA) for intelligible and unintelligible (LP-filtered/buzzed) speech, further broken down by listener group (Orkney and Shetland), assuming fixed factors for presentation condition and dialect (Orkney or Shetland). Figure 4.7 presents the mean judgement scores broken down by speech condition and by dialect.

Examining Figure 4.7, we observe that, for Orkney listeners, there is a large effect of speaker dialect, $F(1,447) = 220$ (p < 0.001), which strongly interacts with presentation condition $F(3,447) = 31.8$ (p < 0.001). The effects for Shetland listeners are even larger, $F(3,472) = 899.6$ (p < 0.001) for the effect of speaker dialect and $F(3,472) = 57.5$ (p < 0.001) for the dialect * condition interaction. As the pattern of results for read speech is largely similar to that of the results obtained for spontaneous speech (cf. Section 4.3 above), speech style (formal versus informal) apparently does not affect the particular intonational features distinguishing the two dialects.[30] Therefore, read speech seems appropriate for this type of study.

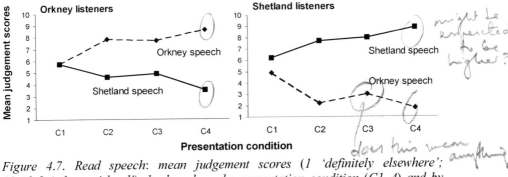

Figure 4.7. Read speech: mean judgement scores (1 'definitely elsewhere'; 10 'definitely my island'), broken down by presentation condition (C1–4) and by dialect, for Orkney (left) and Shetland listeners (right). C1 = LP-filtered & monotonous; C2 = LP-filtered & original intonation contour; C3 = normal speech & monotonous; C4 = normal speech & original intonation contour. Mean data of 19 Orkney and 20 Shetland subjects.

---

[30] Note, however, that for Experiment 1 (Section 4.3, above), the differentiation between the varieties is better for monotonised, intelligible speech (C3) than for unintelligible speech with preserved intonation contour (C2), whereas for Experiment 2 this is not the case. This difference in outcome can most likely be explained by the fact that the stimuli in Experiment 2 were much shorter (1.5 sec) in duration than in Experiment 1 (12 sec): long fragments contain more intonational information than short ones.

4.5.2   Prosody versus segments

This section deals with the role of segmental information versus intonation in the identification of Orkney and Shetland dialects. For the sake of clarity, only the responses for the five main dialect (manipulation) conditions will be discussed here.[31] These are the original but stylised contours for Orkney and Shetland (ORKork and SHsh) and for SSE (SSEsse) in addition to the two hybrid versions, Orkney segments with Shetland pitch contours (ORKsh) and Shetland segments with Orkney contours (SHork). (In the designation of the pitch conditions, the first part of the labels, in capitals, refers to the origin of the segmental information. The second part, in lower case, refers to the origin of the pitch contour.) In the case of SSEsse, the responses are averaged over one stimulus (i.e. one speaker) only; the responses for the other categories are grouped together as follows:

	Pitch contour			
Speaker	ork1	ork2	sh1	sh1
ORK1 **ORK2**		ORKork		ORKsh
SH1 **SH2**		SHork		SHsh

The judgement scores were analysed by two separate two-way analyses of variance (ANOVA) for Orkney and Shetland listeners, assuming fixed factors for speech condition and dialect (manipulation) (ORKork, SHsh, ORKsh, SHork and SSEsse).[32] The mean judgement scores for the five dialect (manipulation) conditions are presented in Figure 4.8. The judgement scores (1 'definitely from elsewhere'; 10 'definitely my island') are broken down by speech condition (buzz, LP-filtered and resynthesised) and further broken down by manipulation condition.

---

[31] The manipulations to and from SSE were included as a control condition only. In the *unintelligible* speech condition, the judgement scores for Orkney and Shetland utterances with an imposed SSE pitch contour were within the same range as those for SSE speech with original intonation; in the intelligible condition, all stimuli with SSE segmental information were judged as being 'from elsewhere' by both listener groups, regardless of the origin of the pitch contour.

[32] All manipulations from and to SSE have thus been omitted from Figure 4.8 (and from subsequent analyses and discussion). The judgement scores for the manipulations to and from SSE are presented in Appendix 8.

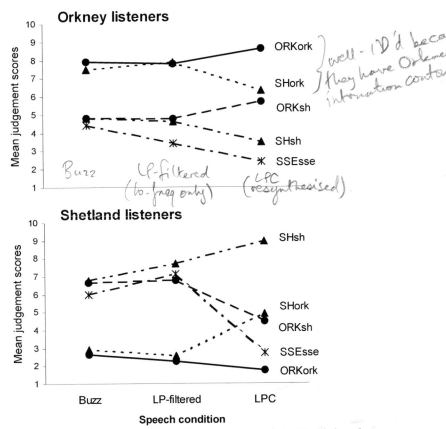

Figure 4.8. Mean judgement scores (1 'definitely elsewhere'; 10 'definitely my island') broken down by speech condition and by dialect (manipulation), for Orkney listeners (top) and Shetland listeners (bottom). See text for explanation of labels. Mean data of 19 Orkney and 20 Shetland subjects.

In Figure 4.8, for Orkney listeners, we observe a large effect of pitch manipulation. Overall, there is a clear split between the topmost two conditions and the bottom three. The former two conditions share the property that they have Orkney pitch contours. The bottom three end up with much lower scores since these have non-Orkney pitch contours. The main effect of pitch condition is significant, $F(4,953) = 192.0$ ($p < 0.001$). A post-hoc analysis for contrasts (Scheffé procedure) indicates that each condition differs significantly from all others ($p < 0.05$). There is a relatively small overall effect for speech condition (buzz, LP-filtered and resynthesised speech), $F(2,953) = 6.8$ ($p = 0.001$). Only the resynthesised and the buzzed speech differ in the post-hoc analysis. However, there is considerable interaction between pitch manipulation and speech type, $F(8,953) = 9.5$

(p < 0.001), indicating that there is greater differentiation among the pitch manipulations in the resynthesis (with clearly intelligible segments) than in the two other conditions (where segmental information is largely obliterated).

The pattern of results for Shetland listeners is almost a mirror image of that for Orkney listeners. Speech with Orkney pitch contours is rejected as non-Shetland, whereas, at least for the unintelligible speech conditions, SSE and Shetland pitch contours receive similar scores. Yet, when the segmental information becomes available, the scores for SSE drop sharply to within the non-Shetland range. The main effect of pitch condition is significant, F(4,1005) = 266.8 (p < 0.001). The post-hoc analysis for contrasts indicates that each condition differs significantly from all others (p < 0.05). The effect for speech condition (buzz, LP-filtered and resynthesised speech) is also significant, F(2,1005) = 7.9 (p = 0.001), but the speech types do not differ from each other in the post-hoc analysis. Again, and crucially, there is considerable interaction between pitch manipulation and speech type, F(8,1005) = 28.5 (p < 0.001).

For this experiment, we used two types of unintelligible speech, LP-filtered and buzz. As we saw in Figure 4.8, the response patterns for the two unintelligible speech conditions are largely similar. From this outcome, we deduce that even when presented with buzz, a signal that does not contain any spectral information, listeners are able to distinguish between intonation systems. Therefore, the conclusion seems warranted that, firstly, the perceptual identification of the particular language varieties can be done on the basis of prosodic cues only, and, secondly, that, at least within the context of the present type of experiment, buzzed and LP-filtered speech can be used indiscriminately.

The judgement scores for the intelligible speech condition (resynthesised speech) are presented in more detail in Table 4.2. The scores indicate that Shetland listeners clearly differentiate between Shetland segmental information with original pitch contours (8.9) and monotonised Shetland speech (8.0) on the one hand, and all other pitch manipulations on the other (< 5.0). For Orkney listeners, the pattern is more complicated, as judgement scores are spread out across the entire range. Speech with Orkney pitch contours, but with Shetland segmental structure, is also classified as Orcadian (i.e. ≥ 6.0).

When in original Orkney speech (8.6) the pitch contour is replaced by its Shetland counterpart, acceptability scores – as judged by native Orcadians – drop by 2.9 points; if the original intonation is maintained but the segments are replaced by their Shetland counterparts, the scores drop by 2.3 points.

Clearly, then, the detrimental effect of replacing the intonation contour is larger (by 0.6 point) than that of replacing the segments.

In the complementary situation, acceptability scores as judged by Shetland listeners drop by as much as 4.0 points (from 8.9 to 4.9) when the original Shetland intonation is replaced by the Orkney pattern. The scores drop to even lower values (to 4.4), however, when the original Shetland intonation is preserved and the segments are replaced by their Orkney counterparts (i.e. a drop of 4.5 points).

Table 4.2. *Judgement scores for resynthesised speech, broken down by dialect manipulation and origin of listeners. Mean data of 19 Orkney and 20 Shetland subjects.*

| Dialect manipulation | | Origin of listeners | |
Segments	Pitch	Orkney	Shetland
ORK	ork	8.6	1.8
ORK	mono	7.7	3.0
ORK	sh	5.7	4.4
SH	sh	3.5	8.9
SH	mono	4.9	8.0
SH	ork	6.3	4.9
SSE	sse	2.4	2.7

The results of Experiment 2, then, reveal an asymmetrical effect. The Orkney listeners seem to attach more weight to intonation than to segments, whilst the reverse seems to be the case for the Shetland listeners. Furthermore, the Shetland listeners seem to react more negatively to Orkney influences, whether prosodic or segmental, than Orcadians do to Shetland speech.

4.6 Discussion and conclusion

The first aim of this chapter was to find experimental support for impressionistic claims that there are intonational differences between the dialects of Orkney and Shetland. The first experiment shows that native listeners from Orkney and Shetland distinguish quite clearly between the two intonational systems when they are presented with unintelligible speech samples in both dialects, i.e. when only prosodic (melodic and temporal) information is available. However, the two varieties were indistinguishable when listeners heard speech that was both monotonised and rendered unintelligible (i.e. LP-filtered).[33] Therefore, the conclusion is warranted that the prosodic difference is a matter of intonation rather than temporal organisation. Furthermore, it was shown that the two dialects also differ distinctly with respect to their segmental structure. The second experiment revealed that, when presented with *unintelligible* speech, Shetland listeners are apparently unable to distinguish between Shetland and SSE intonation contours. In a pilot study with spontaneous speech (not reported here), it was found that Shetland listeners were equally unable to distinguish between unintelligible SSE and Shetland speech. This outcome seems to indicate that Shetland dialect is prosodically similar to SSE.

Secondly, we aimed to determine the relative contribution of segmental information and intonation contour by artificially creating a conflict between the two information sources. The crucial results of our second experiment bear out that the contribution of segments and intonation to the acceptability of a speech sample are roughly equal. For Shetland listeners, segmental deviations contribute more to non-nativeness than does a deviant intonation pattern, an effect that has commonly been reported for this type of study. However, for Orcadians, intonation was the stronger cue for non-nativeness.

Our final, and most ambitious aim, was to present a case where closely related language varieties differ more strongly in their prosody than in their segmental make-up. Intuitively – but so far systematic data to support this idea is unavailable – we believe that dialects, or closely related language varieties, should always differ more in their segmental properties than in terms of intonation. Segments are produced at a rate of between ten and twenty per second, whilst even a simple pitch rise or fall (or combination of both) spans an entire syllable. Except in cases of abnormal tone crowding, then, the number of perceptually relevant pitch changes will be far fewer than ten per second. In addition, segmental information may differ along a larger variety of dimensions than pitch movements. Our results show that, at least for very short fragments of Orkney speech as judged by native Orcadians, foreign – i.e. Shetland – intonation detracts more from its acceptability than segmental information. Apparently, although the cards are stacked in favour of segmental cues, we seem to have found one case of two

---

[33] Similarly, Cohen and 't Hart (1970) found that, when presented with unintelligible, monotonous speech, listeners were unable to distinguish between English and Dutch.

closely related language varieties that differ more in their intonation than in their segmental properties.

At this stage, it is not yet clear how the divergence between Orkney and Shetland intonation has come about. It is not unusual for closely related dialects to differ with respect to melodic organisation. In Denmark, Germany and elsewhere in Great Britain, for example, we also find that many regional varieties have notably divergent prosodic characteristics (Grønnum 1990, Schaeffler and Summers 1999, Cruttenden 1995). In the case of the differences between Orkney and Shetland, the geographical situation (the sea separating the island groups) as well as the diverging histories might have played a role in the origin of the linguistic differences. As Orkney is very close to the Scottish mainland, it is also possible that Gaelic influences, rather than Scandinavian, have indirectly influenced the speech melody of Orcadian, perhaps through Highland English with a Gaelic substratum. In Chapter 7, we shall return to the issue of the origin of the prosodic dissimilarities between the two dialects.

5   A contrastive acoustic investigation of Orkney and Shetland prosody

This chapter describes an acoustic investigation of the melodic and temporal differences between Orkney and Shetland dialects.[34] Typical melodic profiles of short statements and yes/no questions were derived for both Orkney and Shetland speech. Differences were found in overall pitch level as well as in the temporal alignment of the accent-lending rise-fall contours, which are located on the stressed syllable in Shetland but clearly shift to the following, i.e. post-stress, syllable in Orkney. It was also found that the two dialects differed with respect to relative syllable duration. Linear Discriminant Analysis was used to determine which of the three sets of cues afforded the best separation of Orkney versus Shetland intonation patterns. Dialect classification did not exceed 70% when only the pitch parameters were used as predictors. Relative syllable duration yielded about 80% correct, while peak alignment afforded almost perfect, i.e. 98%, correct classification. The results of this acoustic study were found to correlate very well with our earlier perceptual data.

5.1   Introduction

As was demonstrated in the previous chapters, present-day Orkney and Shetland dialects differ markedly in their prosodic make-up. Differences in temporal structure between the two dialects were studied in Chapter 3, and in Chapter 4 it was shown that native listeners proved quite able to distinguish Orkney from Shetland speech on the basis of melodic information only. In this chapter, we present an acoustic investigation of the melodic and temporal differences between Orkney and Shetland dialects. A systematic comparison of the acoustic measurements with the perceptual results presented in Chapter 4 may allow us to isolate potential cues in the melodic systems by which native listeners differentiate between the two dialects.

---

[34] A preliminary version of this chapter appeared as van Heuven and van Leyden (2003).

5.2   Method

5.2.1 Materials

Four short sentences were selected for the production experiment. Two declaratives *There are many gardens in Bergen* and *There are many houses in Bergen* as well as two yes–no questions *Are there many gardens in Bergen?* and *Are there many houses in Bergen?* This type of sentence was chosen in order to permit a comparison with similar investigations, e.g. Thorsen 1978. Furthermore, since no F_0 values can be extracted from unvoiced segments, the sentences were devised so as to contain only voiced consonants.   h ? [ɦ]

5.2.2 Subjects

Twelve male and seven female speakers from Orkney and eleven male and eight female speakers from Shetland (i.e. 38 speakers all together) were recorded for the experiment. The subjects were chosen from several parishes throughout Orkney and Shetland and were between 30 and 50 years of age, having resided locally for most of their lives. They reported no speech or hearing problems and were not paid for their participation.

5.2.3 Procedure

The four target sentences were recorded together with fourteen other utterances of the type *There are/Are there many ... in ...* The stimuli were printed individually on cue cards and presented one at a time; the random presentation order differed per speaker. Subjects were instructed to read at a natural speaking rate and to pronounce the sentences with a pitch accent on *gardens/houses*. The speakers were individually recorded onto minidisc (Sony MZ–R35) in their own home or workplace, each speaker recording the list of materials twice, with a short break between the lists. The analogue output of the minidisc recordings was AD converted (16 kHz, 16 bit) and stored on computer disk for later analysis.

5.3   Results

5.3.1 Measurements

The data set nominally comprised in total 304 recorded utterances: 38 (speakers) * 4 (stimuli) * 2 (repetitions). However, for each of the subjects, only the second recording of the material was acoustically analysed, and only when a speaker mispronounced a particular sentence, which happened in about five tokens, was the first recording used. In addition, the recordings of one male Orcadian were discarded because of excessive creak. Thus, the actual data set comprised 37 (speakers) * 4 (stimuli) = 148 tokens.

Using PRAAT speech-processing software, F_0 was extracted (autocorrelation method) for each utterance. Rise-fall configurations of the pitch accent on *gardens/houses* as well as the accent on *many* were interactively stylised by replacing the original F_0 contour by a perceptually equivalent sequence of straight-line interpolations between selected pivot points, as in van Heuven and Haan (2000), using PSOLA analysis and resynthesis (Moulines and Verhelst 1995).[35] The time-frequency coordinates (in milliseconds and Hertz, respectively) of the pivot points defining the pitch movements were stored together with the onsets of the syllables and the duration of the syllables with which the pitch movements were aligned. No frequency values were entered in those cases where the expected rise-fall accent was omitted from a particular constituent by the speaker. This happened in about twelve instances, each time in the case of *many*. See Figure 5.1 for an example of a stylised intonation contour with associated syllable boundaries and rise onset and offset coordinates.

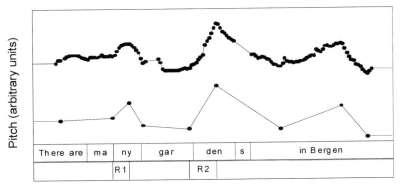

Figure 5.1. Orkney speaker: original intonation contour (top) and stylised contour with rise onset and offset time-frequency coordinates (bottom).

---

[35] In many instances, the Orkney speakers also had an accent on *Bergen*, while this occurred only occasionally in the case of the Shetland speakers. It was therefore decided not to analyse the rise on *Bergen*.

5.3.2 Analysis

5.3.2.1 Intonation

The measured frequency values were first converted from Hz to ERB (Equivalent Rectangular Bandwidth).[36] The ERB scale expresses the relationship between pitch values and human perception and is regarded as the most appropriate scale for intonation studies (Hermes and van Gestel 1991). This scale also allows a direct comparison of male and female speech.

The test words *many*, *gardens* and *houses* differ considerably with respect to their segmental make-up and first-syllable duration (cf. Section 5.3.2.3 below). Therefore, in order to permit comparison of pitch rise location across the three words, it was decided to normalise the alignment of the rises on *many* (R1) and on *gardens/houses* (R2) as follows. The onset of the stressed syllable was given the value of 0% relative time, whilst the offset of the stressed syllable was set at 100%. The onset and offset locations of the pitch rise were then expressed in terms of this relative time scale. Thus, a rise onset at 50% marks a rise the onset of which occurs at a point in time located halfway along the stressed syllable. Similarly, a rise offset at 200% relative time is located two syllable lengths after the onset of the stressed syllable (i.e. a peak located at the syllable following the stress).

Figure 5.2 presents the basic intonation patterns that were realised on the accents on *many* and *gardens/houses*, with pitch plotted in ERB as a function of time, in separate panels for statements (top panel) and questions (bottom panel). The first zero point on the time scale coincides with the onset of the first (i.e. stressed) syllable of *many*; while the second zero point coincides with the onset of the first syllable of *gardens/houses*. In each panel, the intonation patterns of the male speakers are located in the bottom half of the pitch range, typically between 3 and 5 ERB, whilst the female contours are in the upper half of the range, typically between 5 and 7 ERB. Only the rise portions of the accents were plotted. The dotted lines connecting the end of the rise on *many* to the onset of the rise on *gardens/houses* ignore the – highly variable – location of the endpoint of the pitch fall somewhere between the two rises.

The first notable difference between the Orkney and Shetland patterns shown in Figure 5.2 is that, on the whole, the overall pitch in Orkney is substantially higher than in Shetland. Given the fairly large number of

---

[36] Formula (F in Hz): ERB = 16.6 * log (1 + F/165.4).

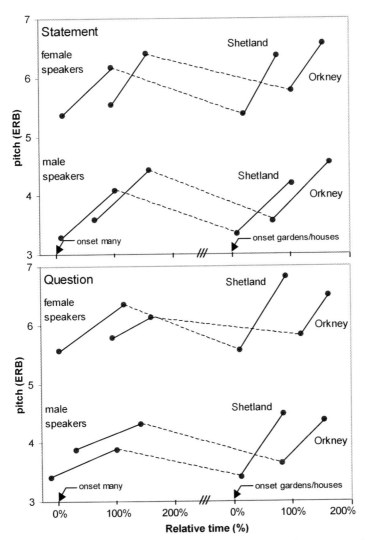

Figure 5.2. Typical rise patterns for statements (top) and questions (bottom), conflated over two utterances, and broken down by speaker dialect and by sex. See text for further explanation.

speakers involved in this study, it seems safe to rule out the possibility that the observed pitch differences are accidental. When individual distributions of F_0 are compared, it is clear that (allowing for differences in pitch between the sexes) there is tight clustering within each dialect community. Also, the fact that the lower pitch in Shetland recurs both in the male and in the female group indicates that the difference is not likely to be due to infelicitous speaker sampling. Rather, we would surmise that the overall higher pitch in Orcadian is a feature of the dialect.

Secondly, we observe that, both in Orkney and in Shetland, the pitch rises have the same slopes and excursion sizes, at least when expressed in ERB, for men as they have for women. Therefore, it seems that the only difference that is related to the sex of speaker is the overall (i.e. mean) pitch.[37]

Thirdly, in statements the pitch rises are roughly equally large (excursion sizes between 0.8 and 0.9 ERB) for *many* and for *gardens/houses*, irrespective either of the sex or the dialect of the speaker. In the question versions of these sentences, the first accent (i.e. on *many*) is considerably smaller than its counterpart in the statement, while the second accent (i.e. on *gardens/houses*) is nearly twice as large, even when expressed in ERB, as the first. It has been shown for other languages (such as Dutch) that the sizes of successive accents increase over the course of an utterance in questions but not in statements (van Heuven and Haan 2000, Haan 2002). In this respect, Orkney and Shetland intonation patterns do not differ from each other or from other languages.

One final parameter that seems to differentiate systematically between Orkney and Shetland intonation patterns is the alignment of the rise. It can be observed, very clearly, that the rise on *many* in Shetland dialect coincides with the first syllable, whereas both the onset and offset of the rise are located at a considerably later point in time for Orkney speakers, such that the peak is located at the syllable following the stress. The same shift in pitch-peak alignment is observed in the rise on *gardens/houses*.

The pitch and alignment data were analysed by separate one-way analyses of variance (ANOVA) for male and female speakers, assuming dialect (Orkney and Shetland) as a fixed factor. The results of these analyses are presented in Table 5.1.

---

[37] The (perceptual) pitch range of male versus female speech is a matter of considerable debate. Although it has repeatedly been claimed that females have a systematically wider range than males, recent studies (e.g. Biemans 1998, for Dutch, and Henton 1989, for English) failed to find gender-related differences in pitch range. Yet, Haan (2002) found that, at least for Dutch interrogative sentences, there are differences in excursion size between the sexes, with women producing larger excursions sizes than men.

Table 5.1. Results of the one-way analyses of variance (degrees of freedom, F ratio, eta squared) for male and female speakers, with dialect (Orkney or Shetland) as a fixed factor.[38] Mean data of 18 Orkney and 19 Shetland subjects.

Acoustic parameter	Men df_1, df_2	F ratio	η^2	Women df_1, df_2	F ratio	η^2
R1 onset (alignment)	1,86	36.2**	0.294	1,48	326.9**	0.874
R1 peak (alignment)	1,86	139.1**	0.621	1,48	35.4**	0.429
R2 onset (alignment)	1,85	134.3**	0.611	1,59	383.1**	0.881
R2 peak (alignment)	1,85	196.5**	0.697	1,59	103.3**	0.628
R1 onset (ERB)	1,86	22.2**	0.205	1,48	2.58	0.052
R1 peak (ERB)	1,86	10.7*	0.112	1,48	< 1	
R2 onset (ERB)	1,85	6.2*	0.074	1,59	6.8*	0.102
R2 peak (ERB)	1,85	< 1		1,59	< 1	

** $p \leq 0.001$; * $p \leq 0.05$

When we examine Table 5.1, we notice that there is a considerable difference between the values for male and female speakers.[39] For men, the effect of dialect is strongest for peak alignment, while the F-values are relatively low for rise-onset alignment. As for pitch level, the effect is largest for R1 onset, whereas the values for the other three pitch variables are very small and, at most, only significant at the 0.05 level. For women, the effect of dialect is markedly higher for rise-onset alignment than for peak alignment, nevertheless the effects for peak alignment are within the same range as for men. The effect of dialect appears to be almost negligible for pitch level. Looking again at Figure 5.2 above, we see that the onset of the pitch rises of both R1 and R2 is located roughly 50 percentage points later for Orkney women than for Orkney men, while the peaks are located at about the same point in time, relative to the first-syllable duration. Consequently, the pitch excursions are somewhat steeper in female than in male speech. No such gender differences are observed for Shetland dialect. In conclusion, we may note that early versus late pitch rise alignment seems to be an important parameter, alongside low versus high mean pitch in the

---

[38] The eta-squared statistic describes the proportion of total variability attributable to a factor.

[39] It should be noted that the group sizes are not equal: 22 men (11 Orcadians and 11 Shetlanders) versus 15 women (7 from Orkney and 8 from Shetland). Consequently, only the values for eta squared allow a straightforward comparison.

case of male speech, for differentiating between the speech melodies of Orkney and Shetland.[40]

5.3.2.2 Syllable duration

A one-way analysis was performed on both absolute and relative syllable duration of the accented words in the test utterance, with speaker dialect as a fixed factor. Relative duration of the stressed syllable of each of the words was expressed as a percentage of the word duration: $Syl_{rel} = Syl_1 / (Syl_1 + Syl_2) * 100$. The mean and relative syllable durations are presented in Table 5.2.

Table 5.2. Mean duration (in ms) of stressed (first) and unstressed (second) syllables and relative duration of first syllable (in % of word duration) for Orkney and Shetland speech. Mean data of 18 Orkney and 19 Shetland speakers.

	ORKNEY			SHETLAND		
	1st syllable	2nd syllable	% 1st syllable	1st syllable	2nd syllable	% 1st syllable
many	138	128	52	174	130	57
gardens	233	186	56	293	175	63
houses	174	157	52	172	145	54

Table 5.2 reveals a clear effect of dialect on both the absolute and relative syllable duration, with Orkney speech having relatively shorter first (stressed) syllables.[41] The difference in relative syllable duration was found to be significant for each of the words (*many*: $F(1,147) = 47.0$ ($p < 0.001$); *gardens*: $F(1,73) = 30.3$ ($p < 0.001$); *houses*: $F(1,73) = 5.1$ ($p < 0.05$)). The effect of dialect was also significant for the absolute duration of the first syllable in both *many* and *gardens* (*many*: $F(1,147) = 66.3$ ($p < 0.001$); *gardens*: $F(1,73) = 30.3$ ($p < 0.001$)), while for *houses* the difference in first syllable duration was not significant. There was no significant difference between the dialects in second (unstressed) syllable duration.

Our results, therefore, demonstrate that pitch rise location seems to have an effect on the relative duration of the stressed syllable; this means that

---

[40] A multivariate analysis (results not presented here), with speaker dialect, sentence type (statement or question) and sex as fixed factors showed a significant effect of dialect (as in Table 1), an effect of sex on rise onset alignment, interacting with dialect, and no effects or interactions of sentence type.

[41] For (unaccented) *Bergen*, the relative syllable duration is 52% for Orkney and 59% for Shetland.

Orcadian, where the peak is delayed until the syllable following the stress, has relatively shorter stressed syllables than varieties like Shetland, where the entire rise is located on the stressed syllable with which it is associated.

5.3.2.3 The role of mean pitch, relative syllable duration and pitch-peak alignment

In order to estimate how successful the three parameters (pitch-peak alignment, mean pitch and relative syllable duration) could be as perceptual cues to the dialect difference, Linear Discriminant Analysis (Klecka 1980) was applied. LDA finds an optimal linear combination of weighted parameter values that allows the separation of data points in pre-given categories. An LDA was set up to categorise the 148 utterance tokens into Orkney and Shetland dialect on the basis of the three parameters that were found to characterise the difference between the two dialects. Since the pitch differs very strongly between male and female speakers, absolute pitch values (in ERB) were z-transformed within the set of male speakers (across the two dialects) and within the set of female speakers (also across the two dialects) separately.

We ran four separate LDAs. In the first analysis, the four F_0 parameters were used to categorise the dialect of the speaker. These are the z-normalised ERB values of onset and peak of the pitch rise on the first (R1) and second (R2) accents in each of the 148 utterances. In the second LDA, only the duration parameters were included, i.e. the relative syllable duration of the stressed (first) syllables, expressed as a percentage of the word duration of the accented words (*many* and *gardens/houses*). In the third analysis, only the alignment parameters were included. These are the locations in relative time, expressed as a percentage of first syllable duration of the onset and peak of R1 and R2. In the final analysis, the pitch, duration and alignment parameters were combined, yielding a set of ten predictors. Since only two categories (Orkney or Shetland) have to be discriminated, the LDA yields a single discriminant function, which is a sum of weighted normalised parameter values. Table 5.3, below, presents the standardised weights that are associated in each of the three analyses with each of the acoustic parameters that were entered.

It is apparent from the results of the LDA that correct classification of the two dialects is moderate when only the frequency values of the onsets and peaks of the rises R1 and R2 are used as predictors. Per cent correct classification is 65% for Orkney and 70% for Shetland, i.e. no more than 20% above chance level (which is 50%). The strongest predictors within the set of four frequency values is provided by the onsets of the rises,

Table 5.3. Weights associated with acoustic predictors in three Linear Discriminant Analyses, and percentage of correct classification for each discriminant function.

Parameter	Pitch	% first syllable	Alignment	All parameters
	Discriminant function			
R1 onset (Z-ERB)	1.003			0.227
R1 peak (Z-ERB)	− 0.266			− 0.229
R2 onset (Z-ERB)	0.566			0.321
R2 peak (Z-ERB)	− 0.552			− 0.230
many		0.818		− 0.112
gardens/houses		0.597		0.113
R1 onset (alignment)			0.111	0.174
R1 peak (alignment)			0.410	0.329
R2 onset (alignment)			0.592	0.527
R2 peak (alignment)			0.620	0.705
% correct Orkney	64.6	80.6	95.4	95.4
% correct Shetland	69.6	77.6	100	100
% correct all	67.2	79.1	97.8	97.8

especially R1, as is evidenced by the larger value of the weight coefficient for these parameters.

Better classification is afforded when the values for relative syllable duration are entered as prediction variables, with correct scores between 78% and 81%. Relative syllable duration in *many* appears to be the stronger predictor of the two duration variables.

Dialect classification is almost perfect with the set of alignment parameters, with percentage correct scores between 98% and 100%. The strongest alignment predictors are associated with R2 alignment, both onset and offset. Examination of the 2% incorrectly predicted Orkney utterances revealed that these concerned three instances of 'mis-accented' pronunciations. In all three cases, the stress-accent was realised on *Bergen* rather than on *gardens* or *houses*, which resulted in an earlier alignment of the R2 onset, but with the pitch peak still delayed until well into the syllable following the stress.

Per cent correct classification does not increase when all three prosodic parameters are combined; the same three Orkney tokens are incorrectly predicted. By far the best predictors of the set of ten are, once again, R2 onset and offset alignment.

5.4 Comparison of acoustic investigation with perception study

The present study allows a straightforward comparison with the results of the perception study described in Chapter 4, in which we found that Orkney and Shetland listeners distinguished quite well between the speech melodies of their native dialect and that of other varieties. Figure 5.3 presents the mean judgement scores (1 'definitely from elsewhere' to 10 'definitely own dialect') plotted as a function of the strongest acoustic parameter differentiating between Orkney and Shetland intonation, i.e. the relative timing of the accent peak. Of course, the mean judgement scores in Figure 5.3 were computed only for those stimuli in which the original segmental information had been replaced by a buzz-like sound (sawtooth wave) that perfectly mimicked the timing and amplitude envelope of the original speech, while obliterating the spectral information. Therefore, the dialect authenticity judgements were exclusively based on the prosodic cues in the stimuli.

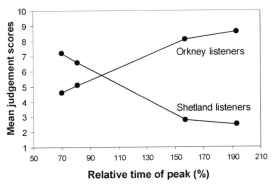

Figure 5.3. Mean judgement scores (1 'definitely from elsewhere'; 10 'definitely own dialect') plotted as a function of relative timing of the accent peak location, broken down by listener group. Mean data of 19 Orkney and 20 Shetland subjects.

The data are shown for the Orkney and Shetland listener groups separately. The leftmost two dots along each line are the mean peak alignment values for the two Shetland speakers whose utterances were the basis of the stimuli for the perception experiment. The rightmost two dots represent the peak alignment values for the two Orkney speakers. We can observe, first of all, the very large effect of the geographic origin of the speakers, showing that early peak alignment is considered characteristic of Shetland dialect and late alignment is strongly associated with Orkney. However, crucially, also within the two pairs of speakers, the individuals are ordered in such a way that the peak alignment corresponds with the authenticity of the intonation pattern. So the effect of peak alignment is systematically found both between and within the speaker groups. Mean peak alignment correlates with the dialect judgement at $r = -0.978$ for the Shetland listeners, and at $r = 0.989$ for the Orkney listeners ($N = 4$, $p < 0.05$). This outcome indicates that the alignment parameter is apparently an important perceptual cue that allows our listeners to differentiate between the two varieties.

5.5   Discussion and conclusion

In the present chapter, we measured characteristic pitch/time coordinate values for the pitch patterns realised on the accented words in two lexically different sentences produced by eighteen speakers of Orkney and nineteen speakers of Shetland dialect. The results indicated that essentially the same melodic patterns were used by the male and female speakers within each dialect. The only sex-related difference was one of overall pitch.[42] This allowed us to normalise for the effect of sex and to come up with a unified account of the characteristic difference between the sentence melodies of the two dialects.

Three sets of parameters were isolated, namely, (1) the pitch values at the onset and at the peak of the accent-lending rises, (2) the corresponding segmental alignment of these pitch points and (3) relative syllable duration. Although the first two parameters seemed to differentiate quite well between the two dialects when we visually compared the averaged profiles (see Figure 5.2), analyses of variance reveal that pitch level differs between Orkney and Shetland dialects for men, but not for women. A token-individual statistical analysis (LDA) unequivocally indicates that the difference between the two dialects resides in the alignment parameters rather than in the pitch or the syllable duration values. In fact, the alignment parameters, especially those associated with R2, afford near-perfect assignment of the utterances to the two dialects. Dialect classification did not exceed 70% correct (a mere 20% above chance) when only the pitch

---

[42] This is, in fact, not entirely true. It was found that for Orkney speech, the pitch excursions are somewhat steeper in female than in male speech. In Chapter 6, below, it will be shown that the shape of the rise seems to play no role in the perceptual identification of the two dialects.

parameters were used as predictors while relative syllable duration proved a cue of intermediate strength, yielding about 80% correct.

The alignment difference between the two language varieties can be characterised as a shift in the location of the entire rise, i.e. both the onset and the peak. The Shetland alignment is 'early', as is normal in most varieties of English and Dutch (Caspers and van Heuven 1993, Caspers 1994). The accent-lending rise in Orkney is 'late' and typically shifts so as to align with the unstressed syllable following the accent. A similar alignment shift has also been found in Glasgow speech (Brown, Currie and Kenworthy 1980:19), Belfast English (Grabe 2002), Donegal Irish (Dalton and Ní Chasaide 2003), Welsh (Williams 1985), Welsh English (Cruttenden 1997:133) and a number of Danish dialects (Thorsen 1978, 1980).[43]

Furthermore, the observed shift in pitch rise location seems to have an effect on the relative duration of the stressed syllable, such that Orcadian has relatively shorter stressed (first) syllables than Shetland speech. An inspection of recordings of Shetland speakers imitating Orkney intonation (not included in the above) revealed that, although they managed to delay the pitch peaks on *many* and *gardens* until well into the second syllable, this did not affect their typical Shetland relative syllable duration. No such recordings are available of Orkney speakers, since intriguingly, Orcadians are apparently unable to produce early-aligned speech.

The results of the acoustic investigation were found to correlate very well with our earlier perceptual data. Shetland listeners regard early peak alignment as characteristic of Shetland dialect whereas Orcadians attribute late-aligned speech to Orkney. This outcome seems to confirm that the alignment parameter is indeed the strongest perceptual cue that allows the two listener groups to single out their fellow dialect speakers – even though the ultimate proof can only be given by an experiment systematically manipulating the accent alignment along a continuum running from early to late, synthesized on a single segmental utterance. In Chapter 6, we will report the results of such an experiment.

Finally, one might be tempted to conclude that Orkney dialect is influenced by its Scandinavian (Norn) substratum. Yet such a conclusion might be false. If the melody of Norn had indeed survived until the present

---

[43] It seems that, at least in unmarked, declarative statements, Orkney pitch accents are comparable to those found in Glasgow and can therefore be analysed as L* H L% (cf. Ladd 1996:143ff, for Glasgow), whereas in Shetland we find an H* L L% pattern.

day, it is difficult to understand why the typically Scandinavian temporal organisation has been lost in Orkney, while it is still found in Shetland (cf. Chapter 3), which does not exhibit the 'Scandinavian' melody. The delayed rises may not be unique to Scandinavian languages and dialects; given that not only Orcadians, but also Welsh, and speakers or formerly speakers of Celtic languages are commonly described as having lilting intonation (cf. references about peak delay cited above), the phenomenon of delayed peaks might be responsible for this auditory impression. If so, delayed peaks might be common to both Scandinavian and Gaelic.

6   Pitch-peak alignment versus overall pitch level in the identification of Orkney and Shetland dialects

This chapter examines the importance of pitch-peak alignment versus overall pitch level to the mutual identifiability of Orkney and Shetland dialects by native listeners of each of these varieties. Using both intelligible as well as unintelligible speech, a range of different test utterances were generated (1) by shifting the location of an accent-lending pitch rise from early to late, (2) by manipulation of the shape of the rise and (3) by altering the overall pitch level of the stimuli. It was shown that in the case of unintelligible speech, overall pitch level was an important cue for Shetland listeners but not for Orcadians. For the intelligible speech condition, there were strong effects of both segmental information and pitch-peak alignment for Shetland as well as Orkney listeners, while overall pitch level played a minor role, but again, only for Shetland listeners. This result challenges the outcome of earlier research, based on solely acoustic measurements, suggesting that the difference between Orkney and Shetland dialects is accounted for by pitch-peak alignment only.

6.1   Introduction

As was explained in Chapter 1, the dialects of Orkney and Shetland are relatively recent developments, based on a shared substratum. However, as we saw in Chapter 3, Shetland appears to have maintained its Scandinavian substratum to a greater extent than Orkney. Shetland CVC words, for example, preserve their typically Scandinavian temporal organisation in that phonetically long vowels are obligatorily followed by phonetically short consonants and short vowels by long consonants, while Orkney dialect does not exhibit this inverse relationship between vowel and coda consonant. Present-day Orkney and Shetland dialects also differ with respect to consonant realisation as well as in lexis and grammatical structure.

However, the main difference between Orkney and Shetland speech appears to be the dissimilarity in intonation. As demonstrated in Chapter 4, native listeners had no difficulty in discriminating between the two dialects when presented with speech fragments containing melodic information only.

In Chapter 5, we found that, both in statements and in questions, the overall pitch level in Orkney was substantially higher than in Shetland. Moreover, it was established that there is a difference in pitch-peak alignment between the two dialects. This difference can be characterised as a shift in the location of the entire rise, i.e. both the onset and the peak. Shetland has early alignment, whereas the accent-lending rise in Orkney is late, such that in disyllabic words with initial stress the pitch peak does not occur on the stressed syllable, but is delayed to the unstressed syllable immediately following the stress. The outcome of a Linear Discriminant Analysis of the measurement results presented in Chapter 5 indicated that the difference between Orkney and Shetland dialects is accounted for primarily by pitch-peak alignment, while high versus low overall pitch is only a weak predictor. However, this outcome does not prove in itself the perceptual relevance of the alignment parameter.

The chief aim of the present chapter is to establish the role of pitch-peak alignment versus overall pitch level in the perceptual (i.e. human) identification of Orkney and Shetland dialects. Additionally, we will investigate the effect of the number of pitch peaks per utterance and also the exact shape of the pitch rises, because whilst investigating Orkney and Shetland speech materials for our study reported in Chapter 5, differences were observed with respect to these aspects of the intonation contour.[44] Spontaneous Orkney speech has distinct rise-fall pitch peaks on almost every word of a particular utterance, while Shetland speech seems to have pitch movements on accented words only. Furthermore, Shetland peak accents are characterised by a straight rise from the declination line, whereas Orkney peaks are preceded by a valley, i.e. the pitch drops below the declination line for most of the accented syllable and then rises sharply into the unstressed syllable. (See also Chapter 4, Figure 4.2.) It should be noted that, at least with respect to statements, the range of the pitch rises is equally large for both dialects.

To address the issues outlined above, identical perception experiments were carried out with native listeners from both Orkney and Shetland. Two experiments will be discussed. In the first of these, the importance of peak alignment versus overall pitch level was examined by systematically manipulating the pitch pattern as well as the pitch level. In the second experiment, we investigated the effect of pitch-peak alignment in more

---

[44] In Chapter 5, these observed differences were, in fact, mentioned only very briefly.

detail, through shifting the peak in smaller steps along a continuum extending from early to late.

6.2   Experiment 1: Peak alignment versus overall pitch level

6.2.1 Method

6.2.1.1 Stimulus materials

The main aim of this experiment was to examine the importance of peak alignment versus overall pitch level. Using an experimental design similar to that of Chapter 4, the utterance *There are many gardens in Bergen* was presented to native Orkney and Shetland listeners. The sentence was digitally recorded by two male speakers, both about 40 years old, one from Orkney (Kirkwall) and the other from Shetland (West Mainland). The recordings were the same as those used in the experiment described in Chapter 4.

Two speech conditions were generated (1) LPC-resynthesised speech (intelligible) and (2) buzzed speech (unintelligible; cf. Chapter 4). In both speech conditions 44 different stimuli, i.e. 22 (intonation manipulations) * 2 (dialects) were generated. The following main types of test utterance were created:

1. Early alignment (the pitch peak is located on the stressed syllable, as in Shetland dialect)
2. Mid alignment (the pitch rise starts about halfway through the stressed vowel, such that the peak is located approximately at the junction of the stressed and the following unstressed syllable)
3. Late alignment (the pitch peak is shifted to the unstressed syllable following the stress, as in Orkney dialect)

It should be noted that the difference in time between early, mid and late peak alignment is unequal. The early peak was implemented always exactly 120 ms after the onset of the stressed vowel, whereas both the mid and late peaks were located relative to the duration of the target word. Thus, in the utterance recorded by the Orkney speaker, the mid-aligned peak on *gardens* was implemented so that it coincided with the syllable junction, which happened to occur 90 ms later than the early peak; the late-aligned peak was realised just before the onset of the [s], which occurred 160 ms later than the mid peak. For the Shetland utterance, the mid-aligned peak was implemented 100 ms later (again coinciding with the syllable junction) than the early peak, and the late peak 110 ms later than the mid-aligned, because of the difference in speaking rate.

The test utterances had either one pitch peak (on *gardens*) or two peaks (on both *many* and *gardens*). Furthermore, two different types of peak were created:
1. A peak implemented as a straight rise from the declination line (as in Shetland dialect)
2. A peak with a preceding valley, that is, the pitch drops below the declination line shortly before the onset of the rise (as in Orcadian).

When the stimulus contained one or two early peaks, no valley conditions were generated, as the valley preceding the peak on *gardens* would have temporally overlapped with *many*. As a result, the stimulus set was not fully orthogonal: instead of 3 (alignment) * 2 (number of peaks) * 2 (peak configurations) * 2 (pitch levels) = 24 versions, only 20 were in fact generated per dialect.

An individual stimulus contained one type of peak only. Each of the manipulations as described here occurred in two versions: relatively low-pitched, starting at 100 Hz, as is normally found for this type of short utterances produced in isolation by Shetland speakers, and high-pitched, starting at 120 Hz i.e. 'Orkney level', giving an increase of just over three semitones in overall pitch. Finally, for comparison purposes, 4 (2 dialects * 2 pitch levels) monotonised test utterances were also included. Monotonisation was done by changing the pitch contour into a flat line. The declination rate for all stimuli was set at four semitones per second, which is about the same as the original rate of the recorded utterances. For an overview of the stimulus types, see Table 6.1.

Table 6.1. Overview of stimulus types.

| | Monotonous | | Early alignment | | Mid alignment | | Late alignment | |
| | *pitch* | | *pitch* | | *pitch* | | *pitch* | |
	low	high	low	high	low	high	low	high
0 peaks	+	+						
1 peak			+	+	+	+	+	+
2 peaks			+	+	+	+	+	+
1valley-peak					+	+	+	+
2valley-peaks					+	+	+	+

Each peak consisted of a straight rise of five semitones relative to the declination line; the duration of the rise was set at 160 ms for both the peak on *many* and on *gardens*. The slope of the fall lasted either until the beginning of the next rise (in the case of the peak on *many*) or until the end of the utterance (for the peak on *gardens*). The valleys preceding the pitch rise consisted of a drop of two semitones relative to the declination line; the shape of these valleys was similar to those found for some of the speakers analysed in Chapter 5. The two-semitone fall lasted 20 ms (two frames) as did the rise. There was a 120-ms time interval between the fall and the rise of the valley in *gardens*. In the shorter stressed syllable *many* the low stretch was absent, i.e. the two-semitone fall and rise followed each other immediately. Example stimuli are illustrated in Figure 6.1.

The manipulated speech fragments were converted from digital (16 KHz, 16 bit) to analog, allowing a signal bandwidth of just less than 8 KHz, and then recorded onto minidisc using a Sony MZ–R35 minidisc recorder. The stimuli were organised into two blocks, one speech condition per block with fragments randomised within each block in the following way: (1) unintelligible and (2) intelligible. In order to compensate for a possible learning effect, two counterbalanced lists were created for each block. Because of the shortness of the stimuli (about 1.5 seconds), it was decided to make each test utterance audible twice successively, with an interval of one second separating the two tokens. The interstimulus interval was 3.5 seconds, offset of second token to onset of first token of the next stimulus; an alert tone was played one second prior to each stimulus onset. To summarise, each stimulus was presented as follows: beep – one second silence – stimulus – one second silence – (repetition of) stimulus – time for participant to write; beep – next stimulus.

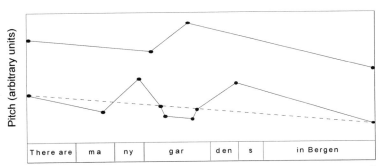

Figure 6.1. Stimulus examples. Top: one early peak; bottom: two late valley-peaks. The dotted line indicates the declination slope.

6.2.1.2 Subjects

Forty listeners took part in the experiment, 20 from Orkney (twelve male and eight female) and 20 from Shetland (nine male and eleven female). The subjects were chosen from several parishes throughout Orkney and Shetland and were between 30 and 50 years of age, having resided locally for most of their lives. They reported no hearing problems and were not paid for their participation. None of the listeners had taken part in any of the other listening experiments reported in this dissertation.

6.2.1.3 Procedure

The subjects were tested individually in their own home or workplace in experimental sessions lasting about twenty minutes including instruction time. The stimuli were presented over headphones (Sennheiser HD 455) at a comfortable listening level. Subjects were issued with response sheets on which they were asked to indicate, for each utterance, where they thought a particular speaker hailed from. They responded by ticking on a 10-point scale running between 1 'definitely from elsewhere' and 10 'definitely from Orkney' (for Orkney listeners) or 'definitely from Shetland' (for listeners in Shetland). See Appendix 6 for a sample response sheet. Subjects were required always to tick a scale position, even if they felt they had to guess. It should be noted that, since the scale had no midpoint, the listeners were always forced to make a decision, no matter how tentative. Preceding the experiment there was a short practice session; responses to these trials were not included in the analysis.

The block of intelligible speech (LPC-resynthesised) was always presented last in order to prevent listeners from transferring information gathered from this block to the unintelligible block (buzz). Each block was preceded by two practice fragments, recorded by speakers other than those used in the experiment; responses to these trials were not included in the analysis.

6.3   Results

A total of 40 (subjects) * 44 (intonation manipulations) * 2 (speech conditions, buzz or LPC) = 3,520 responses were collected; there were no missing responses. However, 40 of these responses had to be excluded from the analyses for the following reason. After running the experiment, it was discovered that there was an erroneous stimulus in the buzzed block. This concerned a low-pitched item with one mid-aligned valley-peak, based on Orkney segments. In the analyses, the 40 responses to this stimulus were treated as 'system missing'.[45]

---

[45] 'System missing' implies that if in a given experiment there is a maximum of 100 responses, but it proves necessary for some reason to have 10 of them discarded as system missing, the remaining 90 responses are regarded as 100%.

Firstly, we will look at the effect of peak alignment versus overall pitch level in the identification process. The effects and interactions of number of peaks, configuration types and the predictably large effect (in the case of intelligible speech) of speaker dialect will be dealt with separately in Section 6.3.2–3.

6.3.1   Alignment versus pitch level

The judgement scores were analysed by separate five-way analyses of variance (ANOVA) for intelligible and unintelligible speech, further broken down by listener group (Orkney and Shetland), assuming fixed effects for alignment, overall pitch level, number of peaks, configuration types and speaker dialect.[46]

The results for the unintelligible speech condition (buzz) are presented in Figure 6.2. The judgement scores (1 'definitely elsewhere'; 10 'definitely my island') for the three alignment conditions are broken down by overall pitch level, conflated over the number of peaks, configuration types and over the two dialects of the speakers.

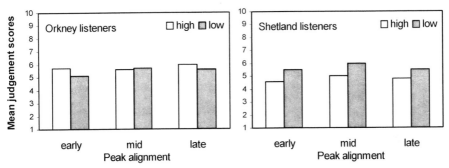

Figure 6.2. Buzzed speech: mean judgement scores (1 'definitely elsewhere'; 10 'definitely my island') for the three alignment conditions (early, mid and late peak) for Orkney listeners (left) and Shetland listeners (right). The results are conflated over two dialects (Orkney and Shetland), number of peaks and configuration types, and broken down by pitch level (high versus low). Mean data of 20 Orkney and 20 Shetland listeners.

---

[46] Although in this section we are primarily concerned with alignment versus pitch level, a five-way ANOVA was used so as not to ignore the effects of peak configuration and type as well as speaker dialect; these effects shall be discussed in later sections.

As can be seen in Figure 6.2, for Orkney listeners, the mean judgement scores for the three alignment conditions (early, mid and late peak) range between 5.1 for early aligned, low-pitched utterances and 6.0 for late aligned high-pitched utterances. However, both the effects of pitch level, $F(1,741) = 2.2$, and alignment, $F(2,741) < 1$, are insignificant; in addition, there is no interaction. Therefore, it seems that the unintelligible speech condition contains insufficient audible information for the Orkney listeners to differentiate between the two varieties.

For listeners from Shetland, the mean judgement scores for all three alignment conditions are consistently about one point higher for low-pitched unintelligible speech than for high-pitched; the effect of pitch level was found to be significant, $F(1,741) = 24.2$ ($p < 0.001$). There is a relatively small effect of alignment, $F(2,741) = 3.7$ ($p < 0.05$), but no two conditions differ from each other in the post-hoc analysis (Scheffé procedure, with $\alpha = 0.05$). These results seem to indicate that Shetland listeners associate low pitch with speech more likely 'from Shetland' and high pitch with speech 'from elsewhere'.

Figure 6.3 presents the results for the intelligible speech condition (LPC-resynthesised). The judgement scores (1 'definitely elsewhere'; 10 'definitely my island') for the three alignment conditions are broken down as in Figure 6.2.

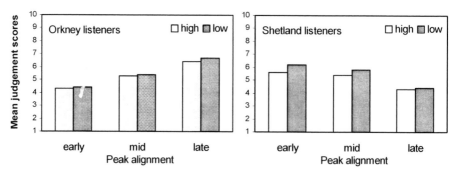

Figure 6.3. LPC-resynthesised speech: mean judgement scores for the three alignment conditions, conflated over the two dialects per listener group. (Further see Figure 6.2.)

Examining Figure 6.3, we see that Orkney listeners clearly differentiate between speech with early, mid and late peak alignment. The effect of alignment is significant, $F(2,760) = 49.1$ ($p < 0.001$). The post-hoc analysis for contrasts indicates that the three alignment conditions differ significantly from each other. The effect of overall pitch level is not significant, $F(1,760) < 1$.

The pattern of results for Shetland listeners is less clear-cut: judgement scores are about 5.5 for both early and mid-aligned high-pitched speech, and around 6.0 for early and mid-aligned low-pitched speech; the scores drop to about 4.4 for late aligned utterances, irrespective of overall pitch level. The effect of alignment is significant, $F(2,760) = 30.2$ ($p < 0.001$). However, only the late alignment condition differs significantly from the other two conditions in the post-hoc analysis. The observed effect of pitch level is relatively small, $F(1,760) = 5.0$ ($p < 0.05$).

Before we continue with the examination of the results, let us summarise the main findings so far. When presented with unintelligible speech, overall pitch level is an important cue for Shetland listeners but not for Orcadians. For intelligible speech, there is a strong effect of pitch-peak alignment for both Orkney and Shetland listeners, while overall pitch level plays a minor role in the identification process, but again, only for Shetland listeners.

6.3.2 Alignment versus segments

Our results so far indicate that, at least with respect to intelligible speech, alignment plays an important role in the identification process. However, as the results for the two dialects were grouped together in the analyses, the effect of speaker dialect (Orkney and Shetland) has been overlooked up to this point. Because of this, we are also unable to compare the results of the present experiment to our findings for natural speech (reported in Chapter 4). Therefore, in this section, we will re-examine the data, looking at alignment versus segmental information (i.e. speaker dialect). The judgement scores were analysed by separate two-way analyses of variance for intelligible and unintelligible speech, further broken down by listener group (Orkney and Shetland) assuming fixed factors for alignment and segmental information.[47]

Figure 6.4 presents the results for unintelligible (buzzed) speech broken down by segmental information and alignment condition, conflated over overall pitch level, number of peaks and configuration types.

---

[47] It should be noted that the responses for the monotonous condition (that is, 0 peaks and hence no alignment) are not included in the analyses.

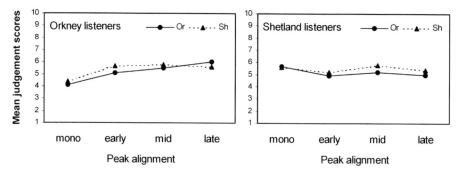

Figure 6.4. Buzzed speech: mean judgement scores (1 'definitely elsewhere'; 10 'definitely my island') for Orkney listeners (left) and Shetland listeners (right). The results are broken down by segmental information (Or and Sh) and alignment condition (monotonous, early, mid and late), and conflated over overall pitch level, number of peaks and configuration types.

The first thing that strikes us in Figure 6.4, is that for Orkney listeners, monotonous speech is consistently regarded as 'least Orcadian', irrespective of the origin of the segmental information. With respect to the alignment conditions, the judgement scores do not differentiate for stimuli based on Shetland segmental information, whereas for stimuli based on Orkney segments the scores range between 5.1 for early-aligned and 6.0 for late-aligned utterances. Both the effect of alignment, $F(2,774) = 1.6$ and segmental information, $F(1,774) < 1$, are insignificant. However, the interaction between the two variables is significant, $F(2,774) = 3.1$ ($p < 0.05$), indicating that the pattern of results is indeed different for the two segmental conditions.

For listeners in Shetland, the judgement scores fall within a very narrow range, although the scores are, with the exception of the monotonous condition, somewhat lower for stimuli based on Orkney segmental information than for those based on Shetland segments. The effect of segmental information was found to be significant, $F(1,774) = 5.9$ ($p < 0.05$); the effect of alignment is insignificant, $F(2,774) = 2.1$, and there is no interaction.

Figure 6.5 presents the results for intelligible (LPC-resynthesised) speech broken down by dialect and alignment condition, conflated over overall pitch level, number of peaks and configuration types.

Examining Figure 6.5, we see that for Orkney listeners, judgement scores for LPC-resynthesised speech range between 3.0 ('from elsewhere') for early-aligned Shetland speech and 8.1 ('from Orkney') for late-aligned

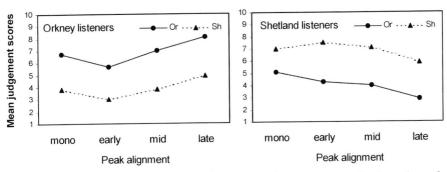

Figure 6.5. LPC-resynthesised speech: mean judgement scores broken down by dialect (Or and Sh) and peak alignment. (Further see Figure 6.4.)

Orkney speech. Given that in natural Shetland speech the accent-lending rise-fall contour is located on the stressed syllable (i.e. early alignment), whereas in Orcadian the accent-lending rise is delayed to the unstressed syllable following the stress (i.e. late alignment), this effect is not surprising. Furthermore, with respect to both Orkney and Shetland speech, the judgement scores are lower for early-aligned speech than for monotonous utterances. Both the effects of dialect (segmental information), $F(1,794) = 334,2$ (p < 0.001), and alignment are significant, $F(2,794) = 53.9$ (p < 0.001); there is no interaction.

As can be expected, Shetland listeners consider early-aligned Shetland speech to be 'most Shetland', whereas late-aligned Orkney speech is judged 'from elsewhere'. Monotonous Shetland speech is regarded as 'more Shetland' than late-aligned Shetland speech. Both the effects of dialect, $F(1,794) = 340$ (p < 0.001), and alignment, $F(2,794) = 33.5$ (p < 0.001), are significant; there is no interaction.

To sum up, with respect to the unintelligible speech condition, the effects of peak alignment and speaker dialect are negligible for both Orkney and Shetland listeners, whereas in the intelligible speech condition, these variables play an important role in the identification process. Moreover, it seems that listeners regard no pitch peak at all (as in monotonous stimuli) as 'better' than a peak that is either too late (for Shetland listeners) or too early (for Orcadians).

6.3.3 Configuration and number of peaks

As stated in the introduction, Orkney and Shetland dialects seem to differ with respect to the number of pitch peaks per utterance as well as peak configuration (shape of the pitch rise). Therefore, the secondary aim of this chapter is to investigate the role of the number of pitch peaks per utterance as well as the effect of peak configuration (shape of the pitch rise) in the identification of Orkney and Shetland dialects. However, with respect to both buzzed and LPC-resynthesised speech, the effects of these variables proved to be insignificant for Orkney as well as Shetland listeners. A very small interaction between number of peaks and alignment was found for the LPC-resynthesised speech condition. However, this interaction is most likely artefactual: the effect of alignment was found to be strongest for utterances with two peaks, implying that two peaks simply contain more information than one.

6.4   Intermediate conclusions

The results obtained so far indicate that, when presented with *unintelligible* speech, Shetland listeners perceive low-pitched speech as being 'more Shetland' than high-pitched speech, whereas for Orkney listeners the overall pitch level is apparently not an important cue. For both listener groups, the effects of peak alignment as well as segmental information are negligible. When presented with *intelligible* speech, both Orkney and Shetland listeners clearly differentiate between the two dialects based on segmental information. Alignment, too, is a very important cue, inasmuch that Orkney listeners regard early-aligned speech as 'less Orcadian' than late-aligned, whereas Shetlanders consider late-aligned speech to be 'less Shetland' than early-aligned. Overall pitch level plays a minor role, but again, only for Shetland listeners. The effects of both peak configuration and number of peaks are insignificant, regardless of speech condition.

6.5   Experiment 2: The role of peak alignment

In Experiment 1, we examined the effect of pitch-peak alignment by shifting the peak from early to late in relatively large as well as unequal steps (see Section 6.2.1.1 above). For intelligible speech, we found that peak alignment played a major role in the identification process. Yet, with respect to *unintelligible* speech, peak alignment seemed to play no role. However, we do not know whether this outcome was caused by the fact that in buzzed speech, a particular peak cannot be associated with any spectral information, or because other variables, such as overall pitch level (high versus low) overruled the effect of alignment. On the same line of argument, the effect of peak configuration (shape of the rise) may also have been overlooked. Furthermore, only two types of pitch peak were included, peak and valley-peak; the third possibility, valley-only, was not examined. In certain language varieties, it seems that it is a *drop* in pitch, rather than a rise, that signals prominence; this feature is reported for e.g. Glasgow speech (Brown et al. 1980:19) and Welsh (Williams 1986). Since for Orkney speech, the pitch drops below the declination line at the onset of the accented syllable, Orcadian, too, could be such a variety. Consequently, in the second experiment we examined the role of peak alignment and configuration by presenting speech with three different types of peak, shifted in small, equidistant steps along a continuum running from early to late.

6.5.1 Method

6.5.1.1 Stimulus materials

The utterance *There are many gardens in Bergen* was presented to native Orkney and Shetland listeners. The sentence was recorded by two male speakers, one from Orkney and one from Shetland; the recordings were the same as used in Experiment 1.

In both LPC-resynthesised and buzzed speech 48 different stimuli, i.e. 24 (intonation manipulations) * 2 (dialects) were generated. The following main types of test utterance were created:

1. a peak implemented as a straight rise from the declination line
2. a peak with a preceding valley, that is, a drop in pitch below the declination line shortly before the onset of the rise
3. a valley only

Each peak consisted of a straight rise of five semitones relative to the declination line. The duration of the rise was set at 160 ms: the slope of the fall lasted 320 ms. The valley preceding the pitch rise consisted of a drop of two semitones relative to the declination line. The two-semitones fall lasted 30 ms, as did the rise; there was a 170-ms time interval between the fall and the rise of the valley. The starting frequency was set at 106 Hz; the declination rate for all stimuli was four semitones per second.

A total of eight alignment conditions was created by shifting the pitch peak from early to late in steps of 50 ms. 'Alignment 1' implied a peak at 50 ms from the onset of the 'a' in *gardens*; for 'alignment 8', the peak was at 400 ms from the vowel onset (i.e. about halfway through the 's'). The eight alignment conditions were the same for the valley-peaks, i.e. the peak was shifted together with the preceding valley in steps of 50 ms, with the earliest peak alignment at 50 ms from the vowel onset. In the case of the valley-only condition, the valley was shifted in steps of 50 ms, so that for each of the eight alignment conditions it coincided with the valley in the eight respective alignment locations for the valley-peak condition. See Figure 6.6–8 for an illustration of the different conditions.

It should be noted that in the early alignment conditions (about alignment 1 to 3) the valley temporally overlaps with *many*, so that there is a pitch drop at the onset of this word – rather than a rise, which would be the normal pattern. Consequently, to both Orkney and Shetland listeners, these utterances may well sound 'odd' and might thus be classified as 'from elsewhere'.

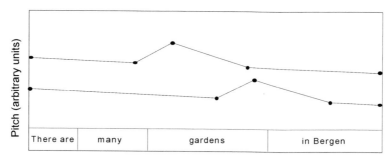

Figure 6.6. Straight rise, top: alignment–1; bottom: alignment–8. The alignment conditions in between were created by shifting the peak from alignment–1 in steps of 50 ms to alignment–8.

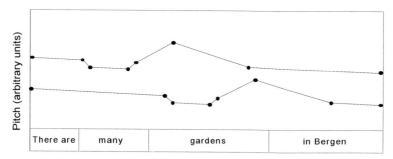

Figure 6.7. Valley-peak, top: alignment–1; bottom: alignment–8. (Further see Figure 6.6.)

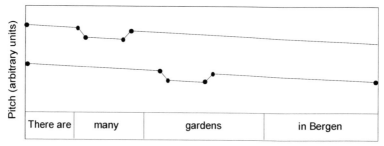

Figure 6.8. Valley-only, top: alignment–1; bottom: alignment–8. (Further see Figure 6.6.)

The manipulated speech fragments were converted from digital (16 KHz, 16 bit) to analog, allowing a signal bandwidth of just less than 8 KHz, and then recorded onto minidisc using a Sony MZ–R35 minidisc recorder and organised into two blocks, one speech condition per block, with fragments randomised within each block. The block of intelligible speech was always presented last in order to prevent listeners from transferring information gathered from this block to the unintelligible block (buzz). As in Experiment 1, each test utterance was made audible twice successively, with an interval of one second separating the two presentations. The interstimulus interval was 3.5 seconds, offset of second presentation to onset of first presentation of the next stimulus; an alert tone was played one second prior to each stimulus onset.

6.5.1.2 Subjects

Thirty-nine listeners took part in the experiment, twenty from Orkney (thirteen male and seven female) and nineteen from Shetland (ten male and nine female). The subjects were chosen from several parishes throughout Orkney and Shetland and were between 30 and 50 years of age, having resided locally for most of their lives. They reported no hearing problems and were not paid for their participation. Although none of the listeners had participated in Experiment 1, some of them had taken part in one of the experiments reported in Chapter 4; these were carried out about a year previously.

6.5.1.3 Procedure

The experimental procedure was identical to the procedure described in Section 6.2.1.3 above.

6.6   Results

A total of 39 (subjects) * 48 (intonation manipulations) * 2 (speech conditions, buzz or LPC) – 7 (missing responses) = 3,737 responses were collected. The judgement scores were analysed by four separate two-way analyses of variance (ANOVA) for intelligible and unintelligible speech, further broken down by listener group (Orkney and Shetland), assuming fixed factors for alignment and peak configuration (shape of the pitch rise).

The results for the unintelligible speech condition (buzz) are presented in Figure 6.9. The judgement scores (1 'definitely elsewhere'; 10 'definitely my island') for the eight alignment conditions are broken down by configuration types (valley, peak and valley-peak), conflated over the two dialects of the speakers.

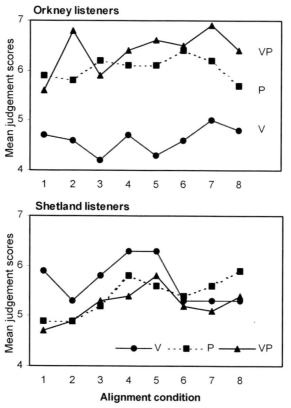

Figure 6.9. Buzzed speech: mean judgement scores (1 'definitely elsewhere'; 10 definitely 'my island') for Orkney listeners (top) and Shetland listeners (bottom). The results for the eight alignment conditions (early to late) are conflated over two dialects (Orkney and Shetland) and broken down by configuration types (V = valley, P = peak, VP = valley-peak).

In Figure 6.9, we see that for Orkney listeners, the scores are lowest for the valley condition and that there is little effect of alignment; the effect of alignment, $F(7,934) = 1.3$, is insignificant. However, there is a large effect of peak configuration, $F(2,934) = 68.2$ ($p < 0.001$); only the valley condition differs significantly from the other two conditions in the post-hoc analysis. This outcome can possibly be explained as follows. As we saw in Experiment 1, Orkney listeners regard monotonous speech as 'least Orcadian'. Speech with valley-only configuration – lacking a pitch peak – is also somewhat monotonous and may therefore be regarded as non-Orkney. For listeners in Shetland, the effect of peak configuration is very small; with respect to alignment, scores are somewhat higher for alignment 4 and 5. There are small effects of both alignment, $F(7,886) = 3.7$ ($p < 0.05$), and peak configuration, $F(2,886) = 2.7$ ($p < 0.05$), but no condition differs from the others in the post-hoc analysis.

Figure 6.10 presents the results for the intelligible speech condition (LPC-resynthesised). The judgement scores (1 'definitely elsewhere'; 10 'definitely my island') for the eight alignment conditions are broken down by segmental information (speaker dialect) and configuration types (valley, peak and valley-peak). Since the judgement scores for the peak configurations are very tightly clustered, it was decided not to label the configuration types separately.

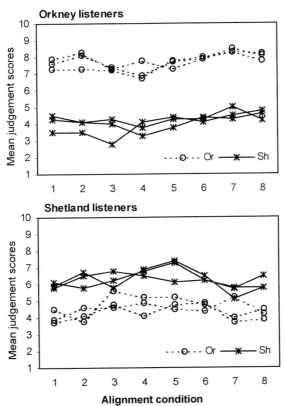

Figure 6.10. LPC-resynthesised speech: judgement scores (1 'definitely elsewhere'; 10 'definitely my island') for Orkney listeners (top) and Shetland listeners (bottom). The results for the eight alignment conditions are conflated over configuration types and broken down by dialect (Or and Sh) and configuration types. Further, see text.

Examining Figure 6.10, one immediately notices that, for Orkney listeners, there is a clear split between the scores for the two segmental conditions, regardless of alignment or peak configuration. With respect to alignment, the scores tend to be highest for the later alignment conditions. Separate three-way analyses of variance (ANOVA) for intelligible and unintelligible speech, broken own further by listener group (Orkney and Shetland), with fixed factors for alignment, segmental information and peak configuration, indicate that there is a very large effect of segmental information, $F(1,910) = 572$ ($p < 0.001$). The effect of peak alignment is small, $F(7,910) = 2.7$ ($p < 0.05$); there is no effect of peak configuration, $F(2,910) = 1.6$, ins. For listeners in Shetland, the effect of segmental information is considerably smaller, $F(1,863) = 142$ ($p < 0.001$). There is a small effect of alignment, $F(7,863) = 3.1$ ($p < 0.05$), with highest scores for the mid-alignment conditions. Again, there is no effect of peak configuration, $F(2,863) < 1$.

6.7   General discussion and conclusion

Two perception experiments, using both intelligible as well as unintelligible speech, were carried out with native listeners from Orkney and Shetland. In the first, we examined the importance of peak alignment versus overall pitch level to the mutual identifiability of Orkney and Shetland dialects by systematically manipulating the pitch pattern as well as the pitch level. In the second, the effect of pitch-peak alignment was investigated in more detail by shifting the peak in relatively small steps along a continuum from early to late. Additionally, we looked at the effect of the number of peaks per utterance as well as the exact shape of the pitch rises in the target dialects.

The first experiment demonstrated that, in the case of *unintelligible* speech, Shetland listeners perceive low-pitched speech as being 'more Shetland' than high-pitched, whereas for Orcadians, overall pitch level seemed to play no role in the identification process. The effect of peak alignment was negligible for both listener groups. With respect to *intelligible* speech, there were strong effects of both segmental information and pitch-peak alignment. Orcadians regarded early-aligned Orkney speech as 'less Orcadian' than late-aligned, while Shetlanders considered late-aligned Shetland speech to be 'less Shetland' than early-aligned. Moreover, it looks as if no pitch peak at all, as in monotonous stimuli, is generally 'better' than a peak that is either too late (for Shetland listeners) or too early (for Orcadians). There were no effects of peak configuration regardless of speech condition; the effect of number of peaks was found to be artefactual. Overall pitch level played only a minor role, and again, only for Shetland listeners.

The second experiment showed that with respect to unintelligible speech, both the effects of alignment as well as peak configuration were negligible. These findings corroborate the results of our first experiment. When presented with intelligible speech, Orkney listeners distinguished clearly between the two dialects, regardless of alignment condition, while the effect of segmental information was much smaller for listeners in Shetland. Somewhat surprisingly, in view of the results of Experiment 1, there was little effect of peak alignment for either listener group. The effect of peak configuration was again negligible.

When asked about differences between the dialects, Shetlanders commonly mention that Orkney speech is relatively high-pitched, especially male speech. Although Orcadians themselves are conscious of the distinctive lilting intonation of their dialect – 'we are always mistaken for Welsh' – they do not appear to be particularly aware of the features of Shetland intonation. The finding that pitch level is a strong perceptual cue for Shetland listeners, whereas, for Orcadians, overall pitch level played no role in the identification process, seems to bear out this native-speaker knowledge. Moreover, it demonstrates that features that are singled out as distinguishing by statistical analysis do not necessarily have perceptual relevance.

When examining the response set for the unintelligible speech condition, we noticed that for female Shetland listeners, the difference between the judgement scores for low-pitched and high-pitched speech was 1.2 points, with the scores highest for low-pitched, while for the male subjects this difference was just 0.5 points. The interaction between pitch level and gender was found to be significant, $F(1,856) = 5.4$ ($p < 0.05$), indicating that the pattern of results is indeed different for the two listener groups.[48] Clearly, Shetland women seem to be more biased towards the Shetland male stereotype (i.e. low-pitch) than men are. The apparent difference between the response patterns of male versus female listeners is a matter requiring further research.

The effect of pitch-peak alignment, reported for Experiment 1 in the case of *intelligible* speech, was expected. In Chapter 4, we found that Orcadians consistently regarded utterances with an imposed Shetland contour (i.e. early alignment) as 'less Orcadian' than speech with an Orkney contour (i.e. late alignment), while Shetlanders considered utterances with an Orkney contour to be 'less Shetland' than speech with a Shetland contour. However, somewhat unexpectedly, virtually no effect of alignment was found for the *unintelligible* speech condition. Yet, in Chapter 4, it was shown that both

---

[48] The judgement scores were analysed by four separate two-way analyses of variance (ANOVA), i.e. for intelligible and unintelligible speech, broken down further by listener group (Orkney and Shetland), assuming fixed effects for overall pitch level and gender.

Orkney and Shetland listeners distinguished quite clearly between the two intonational systems when presented with prosodic (melodic and temporal) information only. The apparent disagreement may be explained as follows. In the experiment reported on in the present chapter, the material was controlled for alignment, pitch level, pitch configuration as well as declination slope. In Chapter 4, we used original pitch contours, which differed simultaneously with respect to all these features. Consequently, important prosodic cues that allow listeners to differentiate between the dialects could well have been eliminated. Moreover, contours were either Orkney or Shetland, but never 'in between', as were many of the manipulations used in Experiment 1.[49] We feel that such a design made the situation rather more transparent to the listener and thus resulted in a clear-cut response pattern.

Given the same line of argument, the absence of an effect of the alignment parameter in Experiment 2 could be due to the fact that a particular stimulus might only differ from the previous one by a 20-ms shift of the peak location. In fact, according to the subjects, the task was extremely difficult, whereas in the case of the experiments with the original pitch contours (cf. Chapter 4) the task was considered quite easy, even when the speech was made unintelligible, and what is more, yielded clear results.[50] In addition, it looks as if the 'valley-only' condition might also have interfered with the recognition process, especially in the case of the Orkney listeners. 'Valley-only' stimuli were consistently regarded as 'from elsewhere' and in comparison, a stimulus with any type of peak – regardless of its relative alignment – might have sounded 'more Orcadian'. Furthermore, in Chapter 4 we found that Shetland listeners seemed to attach more weight to segmental information than to intonation, whilst the reverse seems to be the case for the Orkney listeners. In view of these results, it is surprising that this time Orkney listeners seem to pay more attention to segmental information (cf. Figure 6.10, above) than listeners do in Shetland. To sum up, performance seems to deteriorate considerably when listeners are presented with stimuli lacking a distinctive intonation contour or that hardly differ from each other.

_____

[49] A Scottish Standard English contour was included as well, but as SSE has early peak alignment this contour is essentially the same as the Shetland one.
[50] In fact, as some of the subjects of Experiment 2 had also participated in this particular experiment with original intonation, we can rule out the likelihood that we selected linguistically less competent listeners.

The finding that for both listener groups peak configuration played no role in the identification process again shows that although Orkney and Shetland dialects may appear to differ with respect to the shape of the pitch rise, differences observed by an investigator do not always have perceptual relevance. However, at this stage we do not know whether the failure to find an effect may have been caused because the other variables (alignment, overall pitch level and speaker dialect) overruled the effect of pitch configuration. Therefore, an experiment systematically manipulating the shape of the rise only would be needed to address this question.

7 Summary and conclusion

7.1 Introduction

In this dissertation, we have examined the prosodic structure of Orkney and Shetland dialects. The varieties of Lowland Scots spoken in these Isles are relatively recent developments based on a shared Scandinavian parent language, Norn. Our first aim was to establish whether Shetland dialect has a 'Scandinavian' syllable structure and to see if this feature is unique to Shetland. The second aim was to find experimental support for impressionistic claims that there are intonational differences between the dialects of Orkney and Shetland. To investigate these issues, a series of production and perception experiments was carried out with native speakers from both island groups. Furthermore, the outcome of our investigations was evaluated against results obtained in similar experiments with speakers from mainland Scotland and Scandinavia. In this chapter, we will summarise the main findings and reflect on the origin of the observed prosodic differences between the two dialects.

7.2 Summary and main findings

The investigation reported in Chapter 3 was motivated by Catford's (1957a) observation that Shetland dialect has a 'Norwegian' syllable structure. The essential feature of this is that in stressed monosyllables durationally long vowels are followed by short consonants and vice versa. It was found that, for Shetland speech, a 100-ms change in vowel duration was reflected by an inverse change in final consonant duration of ca 50 ms. In other words, there is a fair degree of compensation in final consonant duration to make up for changes in vowel duration. In Orkney and Edinburgh speech this compensatory mechanism was found to be significantly weaker. In these varieties, an increase in vowel duration of 100 ms resulted in a decrease of ca. 30 ms in final consonant duration. In the case of Norwegian, a 100 ms change in vowel duration was reflected by an inverse change in final consonant duration of ca 60 ms. Therefore, the results indicate that, at least with respect to the inverse relationship between vowel and final consonant duration, Shetland dialect is linguistically a little closer to the Nordic languages than it is to Orcadian or mainland Scots.

A secondary aim of the experiments reported in Chapter 3 was to look briefly at the operation of the Scottish Vowel Length Rule. It was found that, in SVLR-short contexts, the vowel duration in monosyllabic words was about equal for Orkney, Shetland and Edinburgh, while in SVLR-long contexts, vowel duration was considerably longer for all three varieties. In Shetland dialect, vowels were also relatively long in words ending in /d/ derived from historical /ð/ (i.e. a historical SVLR-long context), e.g. *blide* 'happy' (OE *blithe*), *böd* 'fishermen's booth' and *meid* 'landmark' (Scots *meith*). Consequently, in Shetland speech we find contrasting pairs, such as *deed* [diːd] versus *meid* [miːd] and *bide* [baɪd] 'dwell, live' versus *blide* [blaɪːd]. In conclusion, as far as the operation of the SVLR is concerned, the dialects of Orkney and Shetland are neither dissimilar from each other nor from Lowland Scots.

The chief aim of the remainder of the present study was to find experimental support for impressionistic claims that there are intonational differences between the two dialects. In Chapter 4, we first explored the extent to which native Orkney and Shetland listeners are able to distinguish between the two varieties on the basis of prosodic cues. The outcome of a perceptual study indicated that native listeners distinguished quite clearly between the two intonational systems when they were presented with unintelligible speech samples in both dialects, i.e. when only melodic and temporal information was available. However, the two varieties were indistinguishable when listeners heard speech that was both monotonised and unintelligible. Furthermore, it was shown that the two dialects also differ distinctly with respect to their segmental structure. Our results are in line with other studies reporting that listeners are perfectly able to recognise language varieties solely on the basis of melodic information. We conclude that the prosodic difference between Orkney and Shetland speech is a matter of intonation rather than temporal organisation.

The second purpose of Chapter 4 was to establish the relative contribution of intonation and segmental information to the mutual identifiability of the dialects concerned. The results of our study revealed that, when presented with unintelligible speech, Shetland listeners were apparently unable to distinguish between Shetland and Edinburgh intonation contours. This outcome seems to indicate that Shetland dialect is melodically similar to Edinburgh speech. As for intelligible speech, we found that the contribution of segments and intonation to the acceptability of a speech sample was roughly equal. Nevertheless, for Shetland listeners, segmental deviations contributed more to non-nativeness than did a deviant intonation pattern – an effect that has commonly been reported for this type of study. Conversely, Orkney listeners seemed to attach slightly more weight to intonation than to segments. This finding contradicts previous work suggesting that melodic differences are always secondary cues in the identification of language varieties.

Chapter 5 reports on an acoustic investigation of Orkney and Shetland dialects designed to isolate potential cues by which native listeners differentiate between the two varieties. Three major differences between the prosodic systems of the dialects were observed. Firstly, it was found that, for both male and female speakers, the overall pitch in Orkney was substantially higher than in Shetland. Secondly, we found a significant difference with respect to the temporal alignment of the accent-lending rise-fall contours. In Shetland, an accent-lending pitch rise begins at the onset of the stressed syllable, while the pitch peak is located just before the offset of the same syllable. In Orkney speech, the accent-lending rise is shifted to a later position, so that in disyllabic words with initial stress the pitch peak does not occur on the stressed syllable but is delayed to the unstressed syllable immediately following the stress. Finally, it was shown that the observed shift in pitch rise location seemed to have an effect on the relative duration of the stressed syllable, resulting in Orkney dialect having relatively shorter first syllables (i.e. stressed), than does Shetland speech. A token-individual statistical analysis (Linear Discriminant Analysis) was carried out in order to assess which of the three prosodic parameters afforded the best separation of the two dialects. The outcome of this analysis clearly indicated that, acoustically, the difference between Orkney and Shetland dialects rests with the alignment parameter rather than with the pitch or the syllable duration values.

In Chapter 6 we investigated the perceptual relevance of the prosodic parameters that were identified in the acoustic investigation, by manipulating the shape of the pitch contour as well as the overall pitch level. It was found that when presented with unintelligible speech samples, pitch level proved to be an important cue for Shetland listeners: low pitch was associated with Shetland speech and high pitch with Orkney. As for the alignment parameter, the effect of pitch-peak location was negligible for both listener groups. For the intelligible speech condition, there were strong effects of pitch-peak alignment for both listener groups, with Orcadians regarding late-aligned peaks as 'most Orcadian' and Shetlanders considering early-aligned peaks to be 'most Shetland'; overall pitch level played a minor role, but again, only for Shetland listeners. Nevertheless, segmental information consistently overruled melodic cues. In conclusion, the results suggest that, although the difference between the two dialects is explained primarily by pitch-peak alignment, overall pitch level should also be taken into account.

7.3 General discussion

The main conclusion of this thesis is that the closely related dialects of Orkney and Shetland differ significantly with respect to their prosodic structure. This outcome will certainly not come as news to the natives of the Northern Isles, but the dissimilarities have hitherto been described only in impressionistic terms. On the basis of a contrastive investigation of both Orkney and Shetland speech, we have now isolated the crucial prosodic features distinguishing the two varieties.

Our finding that Shetland speech seems to have retained its Scandinavian temporal organisation, while Orkney has apparently lost this feature, seems to confirm the general assumption that Shetland dialect has maintained its Norn substratum to a greater extent than Orkney. In view of the historical developments in the Northern Isles, with Orkney becoming 'Scottified' – both linguistically and socio-economically – much earlier than Shetland, this outcome is not surprising. As pointed out in Chapter 2, there seems to be considerable dialectal variation *within* Orkney and Shetland; however, at this stage we do not know whether the remote varieties (i.e. remote from Kirkwall or Lerwick) are more 'Scandinavian' and/or less 'Scottish' with respect to their syllable structure.

As far as intonation is concerned, we found that the observed melodic difference between the two dialects lies primarily in the alignment of the accent-lending pitch rise. In Shetland this rise is located on the stressed syllable, while in Orkney it clearly shifts to the following, i.e. post-stress, syllable. The Shetland pattern is typical of the intonation of the vast majority of mother-tongue English speakers in Britain. Rise delay, as found in Orkney, is relatively unusual and has not been reported for other varieties of Lowland Scots, apart from the speech of the Glasgow conurbation.

Local lore has it that Orkney's lilting intonation is 'Norwegian' and, indeed, relatively late pitch peaks are also a feature of Scandinavian languages such as Danish and Swedish.[51] Yet, it is puzzling that one should find 'Scandinavian' intonation in Orkney, but not in Shetland dialect, which

---

[51] We are here referring to general peak delay as illustrated in Grønnum (1990), and not to tonemes distinguishing minimal pairs in, for example, Stockholm Swedish (Bruce 1977).

appears to be the more Scandinavian of the two varieties. Moreover, peak delay is also a feature of Celtic languages, like Donegal Irish and Welsh, as well as of varieties of English that have been influenced by a Celtic language, such as, Glasgow dialect, Belfast speech and Welsh English. In fact, there is striking similarity between Orkney intonation and that of Glasgow, which also has 'scoops down in pitch' (Brown et al. 1980) coinciding with stressed syllables. As Orkney is very close to the Scottish mainland (see map, on p. 12), it might be possible that Gaelic influences have indirectly affected the speech melody of Orcadian, perhaps via Caithness dialect. Gaelic speakers, originally from Ireland, appear to have settled in the south and north-west (i.e. along the coast facing Orkney) of Caithness at about the same time as the Vikings arrived in the north-east of the county (Nicolaisen 1982). Although the linguistic frontier separating Gaelic from Lowland Scots speakers in Caithness seems to have remained relatively stable at least until 1700 (Bangor-Jones 1998), pronunciation features appear to have crept from Gaelic into Lowland Caithness as a superstratum (Johnston 1997:447). From what can be gleaned from 1960s archive recordings of elderly Caithnessians, as well as from more recent material, it seems that at least some varieties of Caithness speech also feature peak delay. Regrettably, however, little is as yet known about the melodic structure of the languages that might have affected Caithness speech, i.e. Gaelic and Highland English, nor about possible similarities between these varieties and Glasgow and Belfast English. Furthermore, there appears to be no relevant research focusing on intonation in the dialects of south-west Norway, the alleged place of origin of the Vikings who colonised the Northern Isles. Therefore, we conclude that, at this stage, it is unclear whether peak delay originated in the Celtic languages spoken in northern Scotland or whether the feature should be attributed to the Scandinavian substratum of Orkney dialect.

Shetland intonation was found to be identical to most varieties of English and Lowland Scots in having early peak alignment. However, this does not in itself prove that Shetland intonation might be 'un-Scandinavian'. Until more is known about pitch-peak location in Norwegian, we should not exclude the possibility that in south-west Norway we might find both early-aligned and late-aligned varieties. A prosodic investigation of the dialects spoken in this area would be needed in order to address this issue.

The linguistic situation as found in the Northern Isles is by no means unique in the world. Closely related dialects, which differ prosodically have also been reported for language contact areas such as the Raja Ampat archipelago (Indonesia; Remijsen 2001) and Ireland. In fact, the state of affairs in Ireland is similar to the one found in the Northern Isles. Delayed peaks have been reported for Donegal (Ulster Irish) and Belfast (Ulster English), while not only varieties of Irish spoken in Connaught (south of Donegal), but also Dublin English have early-aligned peaks (Grabe 2002, Grabe and Post 2002, Dalton and Ní Chasaide 2003). On account of this, Dalton and Ní Chasaide (2003) assume that late peak alignment, as found in Belfast and Glasgow dialects is, in the first case, a direct influence of Ulster Irish and in the second case, an indirect influence. To return to the Northern Isles, here we clearly have a language-contact situation too, with Norn and Lowland Scots spoken alongside each other for several centuries, and with the Gaelic-speaking Highlands nearby. Concerning these matters, we agree with Barnes (1991) that a careful examination of the historical developments in the Northern Isles would be needed to gain more insight into the socio-linguistic circumstances surrounding the shift from Norn to Scots.

7.4   Suggestions for further research

The present study has been primarily a contrastive investigation of the prosodic structure of Orkney and Shetland dialects. However, as pointed out in the previous section, in order to resolve the vexed question of the origin of the prosodic dissimilarities between the two varieties one might need to look beyond the Northern Isles. Firstly, we should examine pitch-peak alignment in Caithness dialect, Highland English and Gaelic (i.e. 'the Celtic route'). Secondly, a similar investigation has to be carried out in south-west Norway (i.e. 'the Viking route'), bearing in mind that there appears to be considerable intonational variation within Norway itself (Fintoft and Mjaavatn 1980, Gooskens to appear). Finally, we should compare the intonation patterns of Orkney and Shetland dialects to those found in Norway and northern Scotland so as to establish where the prosodic systems of Orkney and Shetland dialects might have originated.

The outcome of the investigation outlined above might well prove inconclusive since it is by no means certain that Norwegian and Gaelic intonation have remained unchanged over the centuries. Furthermore, if late alignment does indeed occur in Norwegian as well as in Gaelic and the Gaelic-influenced varieties, it would still be impossible to establish the origin of Orkney's characteristic lilt. To address this problem, a more detailed examination of the intonational systems concerned would be needed. As a first step, we would need to examine the structure of the accent-lending rise in the languages spoken in Orkney, northern Scotland and south-west Norway in order to determine which of these varieties is most similar to Orkney dialect with respect to the shape of the rise (or rise-fall). Secondly, it would be worthwhile establishing whether the relevant languages have systematically different speech melodies for declarative and interrogative utterances. In Southern British English, for example, a falling nucleus dominates in declaratives, but not in inversion questions, whereas in Belfast both declaratives and questions have rising intonation (Cruttenden 1995, Grabe and Post 2002). Should it turn out to be that Orkney dialect shares peak delay but no other intonational features with Gaelic and the Gaelic-influenced languages, while at the same time Orkney peak timing, rise shape and also the question intonation are found to be comparable to Norwegian, it would seem likely that Orkney intonation is indeed Scandinavian after all.

At the same time, it is clear that more information is required about the settlement patterns of immigrants from both Scotland and Scandinavia in order to understand the origin of the melodic differences between the dialects of Orkney and Shetland. As mentioned in Chapter 1, previous research focused mainly on the Scandinavian substratum of the dialects, thereby neglecting both the Lowland Scots component and the differences between the two varieties. Consequently, it was not considered essential to pay any attention to the diverging histories of Orkney and Shetland, nor to the precise origin of Scots immigrants to the Northern Isles. Influential immigrants to Orkney from the north of Scotland, in positions of authority, may well have had a far greater effect on the local intonation than might be expected from their numbers. Nevertheless, since late peak alignment occurs throughout Orkney, while early alignment appears to be a feature of all varieties spoken in Shetland, it seems unlikely that the melodic difference between the dialects is a recent innovation.

References

Abercrombie, D. (1979) The accents of standard English in Scotland. In A.J. Aitken and T. McArthur (eds.) *Languages of Scotland*. Edinburgh: Chambers, 65–84.

Agutter, A. (1987) The dangers of dialect parochialism: The Scottish vowel length rule. In J. Fisiak (ed.) *Historical Dialectology: Regional and Social*. Berlin: Mouton de Gruyter, 1–21.

Aitken, A.J. (1981) The Scottish vowel-length rule. In M. Benskin and M.L. Samuels (eds.) *So Meny People Longages and Tonges: Philological Essays in Scots and Mediaeval English Presented to Angus McIntosh*. Edinburgh: Edinburgh University Press, 131–157.

Aitken, A.J. (1992) Orkney and Shetland dialects. In T. McArthur (ed.) *The Oxford Companion to the English Language*. Oxford: Oxford University Press, 731–732.

Árnason, K. (1980) *Quantity in Historical Phonology*. Cambridge: Cambridge University Press.

Bangor-Jones, M. (1998) 'Abounding with people of dyvers languages': The church and Gaelic in the Presbytery of Caithness in the second half of the 17th century. *Northern Studies* 33, 55–66.

Barnes, M.P. (1989) The death of Norn. In H. Beck (ed.) *Germanische Rest- und Trümmersprachen*. Berlin: de Gruyter, 21–43.

Barnes, M.P. (1991) Reflections on the structure and the demise of Orkney and Shetland Norn. In P. Sture Ureland and G. Broderick (eds.) *Language Contact in the British Isles*. (Linguistische Arbeiten 238.) Tübingen: Niemeyer, 429–460.

Barnes, M.P. (1993) Towards an edition of the Scandinavian runic inscriptions of the British Isles: some thoughts. *Northern Studies* 29, 32–42.

Barnes, M.P. (1996) The origin, development and decline of Orkney and Shetland Norn. In H.F. Nielsen and L. Schøsler (eds.) *The Origins and Development of Emigrant Languages*. (RASK supplement 6, NOWELE supplement 17.) Odense: Odense University Press, 169–199.

Barnes, M.P. (1998) *The Norn Language of Orkney and Shetland*. Lerwick: the Shetland Times.

Beattie, A. (2002) *Shetland Surnames*. Lerwick: Shetland Family History Society.

Biemans, M. (1998) The effect of biological gender (sex) and social gender (gender identity) on the three pitch measures. In R. van Bezooijen and R. Kager (eds.) *Linguistics in the Netherlands 1998*. Amsterdam: John Benjamins, 41–52.

Boersma, P. and D. Weenink (1996) PRAAT: a system for doing phonetics by computer. Report of the Institute for Phonetic Sciences of the University of Amsterdam 132. [http://www.praat.org]

Brown, B., K. Currie and J. Kenworthy (1980) *Questions of Intonation*. London: Croom Helm.

Bruce, G. (1977) *Swedish Word Accents in Sentence Perspective*. Lund: Gleerup.

Bryson, B. (1998) Orkney – Ancient North Sea haven. *National Geographic* 193, 46–61.

Caspers, J. (1994) *Pitch Movements under Time Pressure. Effects of Speech Rate on the Melodic Marking of Accents and Boundaries in Dutch*. Ph.D. dissertation, Leiden University (HIL Dissertation Series 10, The Hague: Holland Academic Graphics).

Caspers, J. and V.J. van Heuven (1993) Effects of time pressure on the phonetic realisation of the Dutch accent lending pitch rise and fall. *Phonetica* 50, 161–171.

Catford, J.C. (1957a) Shetland dialect. *Shetland Folkbook* 3, 71–76.

Catford, J.C. (1957b) Vowel systems of Scots dialects. *Transactions of the Philological Society*, 107–117.

Cluness, M.A. (2000) An investigation into the parental influence on dialect acquisition. Unpublished Honours Project, Queen Margaret University College, Edinburgh.

Cohen, A. and J. 't Hart (1970) Comparison of Dutch and English intonation contours in spoken news bulletins. *IPO Annual Progress Report* 5, 78–82.

Crawford, B.E. (2003) Orkney in the Middle Ages. In D. Omand (ed.) *The Orkney Book*. Edinburgh: Birlinn, 64–80.

Cruttenden, A. (1995) Rises in English. In J. Windsor-Lewis (ed.) *Studies in General and English Phonetics*. London: Routledge, 155–173.

Cruttenden, A. (1997) *Intonation*. Cambridge: Cambridge University Press (2nd edition).

Dalton, M. and A. Ní Chasaide (2003) Modelling intonation in three Irish dialects. *Proceedings of the 15th International Congress of Phonetic Sciences*, Barcelona, 1073–1076.

Elert, C.-C. (1964) *Phonologic Studies in Quantity in Swedish.* Uppsala: Almqvist and Wiksell.

Fintoft, K. and P.E. Mjaavatn (1980) Tonelagskurver som målmerke. *Maal og Minne* 1980, 66–87.

Flaws, M. and G. Lamb (1996) *The Orkney Dictionary.* Kirkwall: The Orkney Language and Culture Group.

Friedland, K. (1983) Hanseatic merchants and their trade with Shetland. In D.J. Withrington (ed.) *Shetland and the Outside World 1469 – 1969.* Oxford: Oxford University Press, 86–95.

Gade, J.A. (1951) *The Hanseatic Control of Norwegian Commerce during the Later Middle Ages.* Leiden: Brill.

General Register Office for Scotland (2001) *Census 2001 Scotland.* Retrieved 2004 from http://scrol.gov.uk/scrol/common/home.jsp

Gibbon, D. (1996) Intonation in German. Retrieved 2004 from http://coral.lili.uni-bielefeld.de/~gibbon/Hirst96/german96/

Gilles, P., J. Peters, P. Auer and M. Selting (2001) Perzeptuelle Identifikation regional markierter Tonhöhenverläufe: Ergebnisse einer Pilotstudie zum Berlinischen und Hamburgischen. *Zeitschrift für Dialektologie und Linguistik* 68, 155–172.

Gimson, A.C. (1962) *An Introduction to the Pronunciation of English.* London: Edward Arnold (5th edition 1995).

Gooskens, C. (1997) *On the Role of Prosodic and Verbal Information in the Perception of Dutch and English Language Varieties.* Ph.D. dissertation, Catholic University Nijmegen.

Gooskens, C. (to appear) How well can Norwegians identify their dialects? To appear in *Journal of Nordic Linguistics.*

Gooskens, C. and R. van Bezooijen (2002) The role of prosodic and verbal aspects of speech in the perceived divergence of Dutch and English language varieties. In J. Berns and J. van Marle (eds.) *Present-day Dialectology, Problems and Findings.* Berlin: Mouton de Gruyter, 173–192.

Görlach, M. (2002) *A Textual History of Scots.* Heidelberg: Universitätsverlag C. Winter.

Goudie, G. (1904) *The Celtic and Scandinavian Antiquities of Shetland.* Edinburgh: Blackwood.

Grabe, E. (2002) Variation adds to prosodic typology. In B. Bel and I. Marlin (eds.) *Proceedings of the Speech Prosody 2002 Conference.* Aix-en-Provence: Laboratoire Parole et Langage, 127–132.

Grabe, E. and B. Post (2002) Intonational Variation in English. In B. Bel and I. Marlin (eds.) *Proceedings of the Speech Prosody 2002*

Conference. Aix-en-Provence: Laboratoire Parole et Langage, 343–346.

Graham, J.J. (1993) *The Shetland dictionary*. Lerwick: the Shetland Times.

Grant, W. and D.D. Murison (eds.) (1931–1976) *The Scottish National Dictionary*. Aberdeen: Aberdeen University Press.

Grønnum (Thorsen), N. (1990) Prosodic parameters in a variety of regional Danish standard languages, with a view towards Swedish and German. *Phonetica* 47, 182–214.

Haan, J. (2002) *Speaking of Questions. An Exploration of Dutch Question Intonation*. Ph.D. dissertation, Catholic University Nijmegen (LOT Dissertation Series 52, Utrecht: LOT).

Hart, J.'t, R. Collier and A. Cohen. (1990) *A Perceptual Study of Intonation. An Experimental-Phonetic Approach to Speech Melody*. Cambridge: Cambridge University Press.

Haugen, E. (1976) *The Scandinavian Languages. An Introduction to their History*. London: Faber.

Helgason, P. (2002) *Preaspiration in the Nordic Languages: Synchronic and Diachronic Aspects*, Ph.D. dissertation, Stockholm University.

Helgason, P. (2003) Faroese Preaspiration. *Proceedings of the 15th International Congress of Phonetic Sciences*, Barcelona, 2517–2520.

Henton, C. (1989) Fact and fiction in the description of female and male pitch. *Language and communication* 9, 299–311.

Hermes, D. and J.C. van Gestel (1991) The frequency scale of speech intonation. *Journal of the Acoustical Society of America* 90, 97–102.

Heuven, V.J. van and J. Haan (2000) Phonetic correlates of statement versus question intonation in Dutch. In A. Botinis (ed.) *Intonation: Analysis, Modelling and Technology* Dordrecht/Boston/London: Kluwer, 119–144.

Heuven, V.J. van and K. van Leyden (2003) A contrastive acoustical investigation of Orkney and Shetland intonation. *Proceedings of the 15th International Congress of Phonetic Sciences*, Barcelona, 805–808.

Hewlett, N., B. Matthews and J.M. Scobbie (1999) Vowel duration in Scottish English speaking children. *Proceedings of the 14th International Congress of Phonetic Sciences*, San Francisco, 2157–2160.

Hough, C. (2002) Scottish surnames. In J. Corbet, J.D. McClure and J. Stuart-Smith (eds.) *The Edinburgh Companion to Scots*. Edinburgh: Edinburgh University Press, 31–49.

Jakobsen, J. (1928–32) *An Etymological Dictionary of the Norn Language in Shetland*. (2 vols), London/Copenhagen: David Nutt/Vilhelm Prior. (Reprinted 1985, Lerwick: Shetland Folk Society.)

Jarman, B. and A. Cruttenden (1976) Belfast intonation and the myth of the fall. *Journal of the International Phonetic Association* 6, 4–12.

Johnston, P. (1997) Regional variation. In C. Jones (ed.) *The Edinburgh History of the Scots Language*. Edinburgh: Edinburgh University Press, 433–513.

Klatt, D.H. (1974) Voice onset time, frication and aspiration in word-initial consonant clusters. *MIT Quarterly Progress Report* 109, 124–136.

Klecka, W.R. (1980) *Discriminant Analysis*. Beverly Hills/London: Sage Publications.

Labov, W. (1972) *Sociolinguistic Patterns*. Oxford: Basil Blackwell.

Ladd, D.R. (1996) *Intonational Phonology*. Cambridge: Cambridge University Press.

Laurenson, A. (1860) Om sproget paa Shetlandsöerne. *Annaler for Nordisk Oldkyndighed og Historie*. (*The Shetland Dialect*. Translated from the Danish by J. Nicolson. Lerwick: Johnson and Greig.)

Leyden, K. van (2002) The relationship between vowel and consonant duration in Orkney and Shetland dialects. *Phonetica* 59, 1–19.

Leyden, K. van and V.J. van Heuven (2003) Prosody versus segments in the identification of Orkney and Shetland dialects. *Proceedings of the 15th International Congress of Phonetic Sciences*, Barcelona, 1197–1200.

Lindblom, B.E.F., B. Lyberg and K. Holmgren (1981) *Durational Patterns of Swedish Phonology. Do they Reflect Short-term Motor Memory Processes?* Bloomington: Indiana University Linguistics Club.

Markel, J.D. and A.H. Gray (1976) *Linear Prediction of Speech*. Berlin: Springer.

Marwick, H. (1929) *The Orkney Norn*. London: Oxford University Press.

Marwick, H. (1932) The story of the Islands. In J. Gunn *Orkney: the Magnetic North*. London: Thomas Nelson, 224–262.

Mather, J.Y. (1978) Caithness dialect. *Scottish Literary Review*, Supplement 6 (Language), 1–16.

Mather, J.Y. and H.H. Speitel (1975, 1977, 1986) *The Linguistic Atlas of Scotland*, Vols. I–III. London: Croom Helm.

McClure, J.D. (1977) Vowel duration in a Scottish accent. *Journal of the International Phonetic Association* 7(1), 10–16.

McClure J.D. (1994) English in Scotland. In R. Burchfield (ed.) *The Cambridge History of the English Language*. Vol V. Cambridge: Cambridge University Press, 23–103.

McKenna, G.E. (1988) Vowel duration in the Standard English of Scotland. Unpublished M. Litt. dissertation, University of Edinburgh.

Melchers, G. (1981) The Norn element in Shetland dialect today – a case of "never-accepted" language death. In E. Ejerhed and I. Henrysson (eds.) *Tvåspråkighet.* (Umeå studies in the Humanities 36.) Umeå: University of Umeå, 254–261.

Melchers, G. (1984) Is the structure of the syllable in Shetland dialect "Scandinavian"? In C.-C. Elert, I. Johansson and E. Strangert (eds.) *Nordic Prosody III.* (Umeå Studies in the Humanities 59.) Umeå: University of Umeå, 179–186.

Melchers, G. (1985) 'Knappin', 'proper English', 'modified Scots' Some language attitudes in the Shetland Isles. In M. Görlach (ed.) *Focus on Scotland.* Amsterdam: John Benjamins, 87–100.

Melchers, G. (1992) "Du's no heard da last o'dis"– on the use of *be* as a perfective auxiliary in Shetland dialect. In M. Riisanen (ed.) *History of Englishes: New Methods and Interpretations in Historical Linguistics.* Berlin: Mouton de Gruyter, 602–610.

Moulines, E. and W. Verhelst (1995) Time-domain and frequency-domain techniques for prosodic modification of speech. In W.B. Kleijn and K.K. Paliwal (eds.) *Speech Coding and Synthesis.* Amsterdam: Elsevier Science, 519–555.

Nicolaisen, W.F.H. (1982) Scandinavians and Celts in Caithness: the place-name evidence. In J.R. Baldwin (ed.) *Caithness: A Cultural Crossroads.* Edinburgh: Scottish Society for Northern Studies, 75–85.

Nooteboom, S.G. (1997) The prosody of speech: Melody and rhythm. In W.J. Hardcastle and J. Laver (eds.) *The Handbook of Phonetic Sciences.* Oxford: Blackwell, 640–673.

Norquay, T. (2003) Is the consonant system of Orcadian changing? An apparent-time group study. Unpublished Honours Project, Queen Margaret University College, Edinburgh.

Ohala, J.J. and J.B. Gilbert (1980) Listeners' ability to identify languages by their prosody. In P. Léon and M. Rossi (eds.) *Problèmes de Prosodie II: Expérimentations, modèles et fonctions.* Ottawa: Didier, 123–131.

O'Hanlon, R. (2003) *Trawler. A Journey Through the North Atlantic.* London: Hamish Hamilton.

Pálsson, H. and P. Edwards (1978) *Orkneyinga Saga: The History of the Earls of Orkney.* London: Hogarth Press.

Pavlenko, A. (1997) The origin of the *be*-perfect with transitives in the Shetland dialect. *Scottish Language* 16, 88–96.

Peters, J., P. Gilles, P. Auer and M. Selting (2002) Identification of regional varieties by intonational cues. An experimental study on Hamburg and Berlin German. *Language and Speech*, 45, 115–139.

Peters, J., P. Gilles, P. Auer and M. Selting (2003) Identifying regional varieties by pitch information: A comparison of two approaches. *Proceedings of the 15th International Congress of Phonetic Sciences*, Barcelona, 1065–1068.

Peterson, G.E. and I. Lehiste (1960) Duration of syllable nuclei in English. *Journal of the Acoustical Society of America* 32, 693–703.

Remijsen, B. (2001) *Word-prosodic Systems of the Raja Ampat Languages*. Ph.D. dissertation, Leiden University (LOT Dissertation Series 49, Utrecht: LOT).

Rendboe, L. (1984) How "worn out" or "corrupted" was Shetland Norn in its final stage? *NOWELE* 3, 53–88.

Rendboe, L. (1993) Low's last local Norn text from Shetland 1774. *NOWELE* 21/22, 117–136.

Schaeffler, F. and R. Summers (1999) Recognizing German dialects by prosodic features alone. *Proceedings of the 14th International Congress of Phonetic Sciences*, San Francisco, 2311–2314.

Scobbie, J.M. (to appear) Flexibility in the face of incompatible English VOT systems. In L. Goldstein and C. T. Best *Laboratory Phonology VIII*. Berlin: Mouton de Gruyter.

Scobbie, J.M., A.E. Turk and N. Hewlett (1999) Morphemes, phonetics and lexical items: the case of the Scottish Vowel Length Rule. *Proceedings of the 14th International Congress of Phonetic Sciences*, San Francisco, 1617–1620.

Smith, B. (1996) The development of the spoken and written Shetland dialect: a historians view. In D.J. Waugh (ed.) *Shetland's Northern Links: Language and History*. Edinburgh: Scottish Society for Northern Studies, 30–43.

Smith, B. (2001) The Picts and the martyrs or did Vikings kill the native population of Orkney and Shetland. *Northern Studies* 36, 7–32.

Stewart, J. (1987) *Shetland Place-Names*. Lerwick: Shetland Library and Museum.

Stewart, J. (1964) Norn in Shetland. *Fróðskapparit* 13, 158–175.

Strangert, E. (2001) Quantity in ten Swedish dialects in Northern Sweden and Österbotten in Finland. *Lund University, Dept. of Linguistics Working Papers* 49, 144–147.

Tench, P. (1990) The pronunciation of English in Abercrave. In N. Coupland *English in Wales: Diversity, Conflict and Change*. Clevedon/ Philadelphia: Multilingual Matters, 130–141.

Thomson, W.P.L. (2001) *The New History of Orkney*. Edinburgh: Mercat Press.

Thorsen, N. (1978) An acoustical investigation of Danish intonation. *Journal of Phonetics* 6, 151–175.

Thorsen, N. (1980) A study on the intonation of sentence intonation – evidence from Danish. *Journal of the Acoustical Society of America*, 67, 1014–1030.

Thorsen, P. (1954) The third Norn dialect – that of Caithness. In W.D. Simpson (ed.) *Viking Congress Lerwick, July 1950*. Edinburgh: Aberdeen University Studies, 230–238.

Trudgill, P. and J. Hannah (1982) *International English*. London: Edward Arnold.

Wales, K. (to appear) Second person pronouns in contemporary English: The end of a story of just the beginning? *Journal of Franco-British Studies*.

Waugh, D.J. (1989) Place-names. In D. Omand (ed.) *The New Caithness Book*. Wick: North of Scotland Newspapers, 141–155.

Wells, J.C. (1982) *Accents of English* I–III. Cambridge: Cambridge University Press.

Willems, N. (1982) *English Intonation from a Dutch Point of View*. Dordrecht: Foris.

Williams, B. (1985) Pitch and duration in Welsh stress perception: the implications for intonation. *Journal of Phonetics* 13, 381–406.

Appendices

Appendix 1. Test words for Shetland, Orkney and Edinburgh (Chapter 3).[52][53]

VOWEL CLASS

	meet	beat	mate	bait	bet	bit	boot	out
Older Scots	e:	ɛ:	a:	ai	ɛ	ɪ	ø	u:
Northern Isles	i	e, i	e, ɛ	e, ɛ	ɛ, e	ë, ɪ	ø	u
Lexical set (cf. Wells 1982)	*meet*	*beat*	*mate*	*bait*	*bet*	*bit*	*boot*	*out*
Final consonant								
#	bee	pea	toe	day	*	*	do	coo
b	Beeb					bib		
d	deed			maed		kid	guid	
	meid			saed			böd	
g	league					big		
p	deep					dip		
t	beet	beat	mate	bait	met	bit	boot	doot
k	seek					tick		
f	beef					stiff		
v	reeve					sieve		
s	piece					kiss		
z	seize					Liz		
l	keel					kill	buil	
							bruil	
r	beer	fear	more	pair	Kerr	fir	poor	soor
tʃ	beech					pitch		
θ	Keith					pith		
ð	seethe							
ʃ	quiche					dish		
m	teem	team	tame	aim	stem	dim	tume	doom
n	keen		hain	pain	hen	kin		
					pen			
ŋ	*					king		
#ed	tee'd					*		
#pl	tees					*		

[52] For selection criteria and further explanation, see Chapter 3, section 3.2.1.

[53] The spelling of Scottish dialect words in this table confirms to the spelling as used in the *Scottish National Dictionary*; Shetland dialect words, which are not listed in the *SND* as well as Scottish words which are pronounced differently in Shetland than elsewhere in Scotland, are spelled according to the Shetland dictionary (Graham 1993).

Test words for Shetland, Orkney and Edinburgh. (*Continued*)

	VOWEL CLASS									
Older Scots	ʊ	ɔː	ɔ	au	a	iː	iː	ɔi	ɔu	ɛu
Northern Isles	ŏ	ɒ, ɔ, o	ɒ	ɑ, a	a	ɜi	ai	ɒi	ŏu	ju
Lexical set	*cut*	*coat*	*cot*	*caught*	*cat*	*bite*	*try*	*voice*	*loup*	*dew*
Final consonant										
#	*	doh	*	ba	*	*	kye	toy	knowe	dew
b										
d				fraud	bad	bide	blide			
g				claag	clag					
p										
t	cut	boat	pot	faut	fat	kite	*		nowt	newt
k				bauk	back					
f										
v										
s										
z										
l										
r	fur	boar		waar	bar	*	fire		four	
tʃ										
θ										
ð										
ʃ										
m	gum	foam	bomb	calm	palm	time	*			
n										
ŋ										
#ed										
#pl										

Glossary

bauk	wooden beam, hen roost		ba	ball
böd	a small house in which fishing tackle is kept (ON *būð*)		bauk	baulk
bruil	bellow (n,v) (Norw. *braula*)		blide	blithe
buil	resting place for animals, nest (ON *ból*)		clag	to clog
claag	to gossip, to chatter (Sc. *to claik*)		coo	cow
hain	to use sparingly (ON *hegna*)		doot	doubt
maed	maggot (OE *maþa*)		faut	fault
meid	landmark, seamark (Sc. *meith*, ON *mið*)		guid	good
saed	coalfish (Sc. saithe, ON *seiðr*)		kye	cows
steid	foundation (Sc. stead, ON *staðr*)		nowt	nought
tume	to empty (ON *tœma*)		soor	sour
waar	seaweed (OE *war*)			

Test words for Shetland, Orkney and Edinburgh. (*Continued*)

In several cases, alternative test words were necessary because a number of the words we wished to examine in the Shetland version of the experiment either do not occur in present-day Orkney or Edinburgh speech, or are pronounced somewhat differently.

Orkney alternatives:

bauk = baulk	claag = claik	faut = fault	maed = maid
meid = steid	saed = saithe		

Edinburgh alternatives:

ba = ball	claag = claik	guid = good	saed = saithe
bauk = baulk	clag = clog	hain = vain	soor = sour
böd = booth	coo = cow	maed = maid	tume = Tom
bruil = brill	doot = doubt	meid = steed	waar = ware
buil = bill	faut = fault	nowt = nought	

Appendix 2. Test words for Norwegian (Chapter 3)

	/y:/–/y/	English	/ø:/– /ø/	English	/a:/–/a/	English
/t/	flyt	flow	søt	sweet	mat	food
/t:/	nytt	news	nøtt	nut	matt	dull
/k/	syk	ill	bøk	beech	tak	roof
/k:/	tykk	thick	møkk	muck	takk	thanks
/n/	syn	sight	føn	föhn	man	mane
/n:/	tynn	thin	sønn	son	mann	man
/l/	syl	awl	døl	dalesman	dal	valley
/l:/	fyll	filling	møll	moth	pall	pallet
/s/	nys	sneeze	døs	doze	mas	hassle
/s:/	nyss	hint	bøss	dirt	bass	bass

	/ɛ/–/e:/	English	/i/–/i:/	English
/t/	fet	fat	bit	bit
/t:/	sett	set	bitt	a bite
/k/	bek	pitch	vik	bay, inlet
/k:/	bekk	brook	nikk	nod
/n/	ben	bone	fin	fine
/n:/	penn	penn	finn	find
/l/	del	part	bil	car
/l:/	fell	skin	dill	dill
/s/	nes	ness	dis	fog
/s:/	gress	grass	piss	urine

Appendix 3: The relationship between vowel and final consonant duration in Dutch (Chapter 3)

In order to find out if, and to what extent, the compensatory mechanism as found in Shetland dialect occurs in non-Scandinavian Germanic languages, a control experiment was conducted with five Dutch speakers (Rotterdam area). Dutch has free and checked vowels, which have a durational relationship (checked vowels being durationally short and free vowels generally longer).[54] Thirty-two Monosyllabic Dutch –VC words were read in the carrier phrase *Ik zei* [*woord*] *altijd* 'I said [word] always'. Segment durations of the target words were measured using the same criteria as for the experiments in chapter 3.

The product-moment correlation between vowel and final consonant duration for the 32 measured Dutch –VC words is –0.715 for words with final /–s, –p, –m/ (–0.658 for words final /–t/). The regression function predicting C^f duration from V duration $C^f_i = (V_i*-0.156) + 103$. Hence, in Dutch, a 100 ms increase in vowel duration results in a decrease of just 16 ms in final consonant duration.

---

[54] The free vowels /i,y,u/ are exceptions; except before /r/, they are typically short.

Appendix 4: Transcripts of speech fragments (Chapter 4, Exp. 1)

Orkney 1

There was no a ... they would maybe have a sitting room, you ken, but nobody would ever go in the sitting room, because it was always cold ... Might have nice seats and might even have a carpet in that bit o' the hoose, but nobody would be in it.

Orkney 2

If it's somebody I know, and in the family, I'm very broad ... and ... and relaxed, but as soon as anybody can't hear me or doesn't understand me, we automatically change to something closer to what we hear on TV or ... a more understandable English.

Orkney 3

I got home on a Friday night, and by Monday I'd hen 'had' two phone calls offering me jobs and ... withoot applying, I mean ... folk would just gotten to know that I was going to be out o' work and I ... I ... they phoned and asked if I wanted to work.

Shetland 1

We're away for a week; we have four of a crew and we change crews every week; we come home and another four men goes to sea ... and we get the same pay the week you're home as the week you're at sea.

Shetland 2

But it can be very unfortunate for the folk, because very often when you're moved into your new hoose, you buy all new curtains and carpets and stuff, and they feel as if it's just been violated by the flechs 'flees'.

Shetland 3

There could be a couple o' spaces, but we would have to sit in the ... emergency seat and somebody sitting wi' the pilot, but first they'd have to weigh wis 'us' and when the lighthoose board man went on the scale, that was no bother, but when I went on...

Appendix 5:   Illustration of speech types (Chapter 4, Exp. 1)

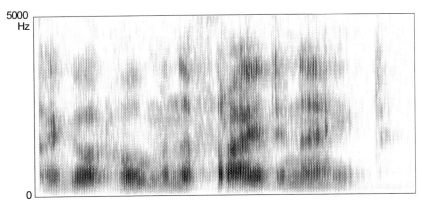

Spectrogram of 'I got home on a Friday night...' (normal speech).

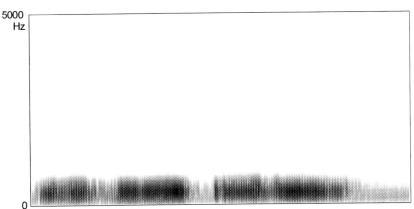

Spectrogram of 'I got home on a Friday night...' (LP-filtered speech).

Appendix 6: Sample response sheet (Chapter 4 and 6)

List 1

	from elsewhere					from Orkney				
sentence 1	1	2	3	4	5	6	7	8	9	10
sentence 2	1	2	3	4	5	6	7	8	9	10
sentence 3	1	2	3	4	5	6	7	8	9	10
sentence 4	1	2	3	4	5	6	7	8	9	10
sentence 5	1	2	3	4	5	6	7	8	9	10
sentence 6	1	2	3	4	5	6	7	8	9	10
sentence 7	1	2	3	4	5	6	7	8	9	10
sentence 8	1	2	3	4	5	6	7	8	9	10
sentence 9	1	2	3	4	5	6	7	8	9	10
sentence 10	1	2	3	4	5	6	7	8	9	10
sentence 11	1	2	3	4	5	6	7	8	9	10
sentence 12	1	2	3	4	5	6	7	8	9	10
sentence 13	1	2	3	4	5	6	7	8	9	10
sentence 14	1	2	3	4	5	6	7	8	9	10
sentence 15	1	2	3	4	5	6	7	8	9	10
sentence 16	1	2	3	4	5	6	7	8	9	10
sentence 17	1	2	3	4	5	6	7	8	9	10
sentence 18	1	2	3	4	5	6	7	8	9	10

Appendix 7:   Illustration of speech types (Chapter 4, Exp. 2)

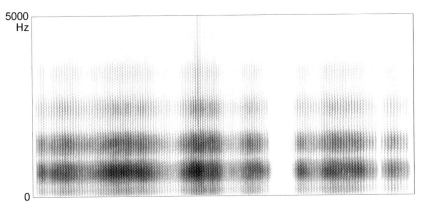

Spectrogram of 'There are many gardens in Bergen' (buzzed speech).

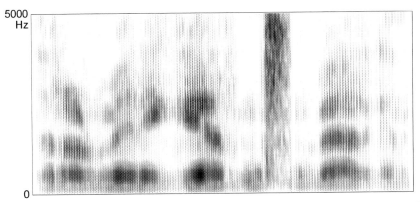

Spectrogram of 'There are many gardens in Bergen' (LPC-resynthesised speech).

Appendix 8: Judgement scores for the manipulations to and from SSE together with those of the monotonised utterances (Chapter 4, Exp. 2)

Judgement scores for the three speech conditions, broken down by dialect manipulation and origin of listeners. Mean data of 19 Orkney and 20 Shetland subjects. See Chapter 4, Section 4.5.2 for further explanation.

Buzzed speech			
Dialect manipulation		*Origin of listeners*	
Segments	**Pitch**	**Orkney**	**Shetland**
ORK	sse	5.2	6.0
SH	sse	5.4	5.4
SSE	ork	7.1	3.2
SSE	sh	4.4	6.7
SSE	mono	5.3	5.9

LP-filtered speech			
Dialect manipulation		*Origin of listeners*	
Segments	**Pitch**	**Orkney**	**Shetland**
ORK	sse	4.3	6.6
SH	sse	4.4	7.8
SSE	ork	7.2	2.5
SSE	sh	4.1	6.6
SSE	mono	4.9	5.8

LPC speech			
Dialect manipulation		*Origin of listeners*	
Segments	**Pitch**	**Orkney**	**Shetland**
ORK	sse	6.4	4.2
SH	sse	3.9	8.8
SSE	ork	3.6	2.1
SSE	sh	2.2	2.5
SSE	mono	2.6	3.3

Samenvatting in het Nederlands

De Orkney en Shetland eilanden – gelegen ten noorden van het Schotse vasteland – zijn in de negende eeuw gekoloniseerd door Vikingen uit Noorwegen. Het lot van de oorspronkelijke bevolking van de eilanden is omstreden, maar het meest waarschijnlijke scenario is dat ze is uitgeroeid door de invallers. De taal die werd gesproken door de nieuwkomers en hun nakomelingen raakte bekend als het Norn en dit Scandinavische dialect zou tot ver na de Vikingtijd de belangrijkste voertaal blijven. Orkney en Shetland stonden onder Scandinavisch gezag tot 1468–69 toen de eilanden door de koning van Denemarken en Noorwegen werden verpand aan het Schotse koningshuis als borg voor de bruidsschat van zijn dochter. Orkney onderhield al sinds de twaalfde eeuw nauwe contacten met het nabijgelegen Schotse vasteland, maar na de machtsoverdracht begint ook het verder afgelegen Shetland zich meer en meer op Schotland te richten. In de loop der tijd vestigen zich steeds meer Engels sprekende ambtenaren en gezags-bekleders op Orkney en Shetland, waardoor de eilanden tweetalig worden: in formele situaties is het Engels de voertaal, terwijl er door de oorspronkelijke bewoners thuis Norn wordt gesproken. In de loop van de achttiende eeuw zal het Norn uiteindelijk definitief plaats maken voor het Schotse Engels.

In de dialecten die thans gesproken worden op de Orkney en Shetland eilanden, is de invloed van het Norn nog duidelijk merkbaar in zowel de woordenschat, de grammatica alsook de uitspraak. Volgens Catford (1957a) heeft het dialect van Shetland bovendien zijn oorspronkelijke Scandinavische lettergreepstructuur behouden. Deze structuur houdt in dat eenlettergrepige woorden die eindigen in een medeklinker óf een korte klinker hebben die gevolgd wordt door een lange slotmedeklinker (als in *pott*), óf een lange klinker gevolgd door een korte slotmedeklinker (als in *boat*). Een dergelijke inverse relatie tussen klinker en slotmedeklinker vinden we ook terug in het hedendaagse Noors en Zweeds. Wat betreft de intonatie (dat wil zeggen, de spraakmelodie) zou er volgens de eilandbewoners eveneens een verwant-schap bestaan tussen hun dialect en het Noors. Een probleem bij deze bewering is echter dat de intonatiesystemen van de twee dialecten nogal van elkaar lijken te verschillen: het dialect van Orkney klinkt erg zangerig terwijl het Shetlands wat monotoon overkomt. De intonatie van het Orcadian en het

Shetlands is tot op heden niet bestudeerd en ook is er nauwelijks onderzoek gedaan naar de verschillen tussen de twee dialecten.

Het doel van hoofdstuk 3 van dit proefschrift was om vast te stellen of het Shetlands anno 2000 nog steeds zijn Scandinavische lettergreepstructuur heeft behouden en in hoeverre de Shetlandse lettergreep wat dit betreft verschilt (of misschien overeenkomt) met die van het Orcadian, het Noors en het Schotse Engels zoals dat in Edinburgh gesproken wordt. Voor dit onderzoek hebben we een reeks geluidsopnames gemaakt van moedertaal-sprekers van deze vier taalvariëteiten. Elke proefpersoon las een identieke lijst voor met woorden van het type *deep*, *big* en *time*; de Noorse sprekers lazen soortgelijke woorden, maar dan in hun eigen taal. Om er voor te zorgen dat de woorden met een gelijkmatige snelheid werden uitgesproken waren ze ingebed in de draagzin *I say ... again* (*Jeg sa ... alltid* voor de Noren). De metingen aan de testwoorden leveren de volgende resultaten op. In het Shetlands wordt een klinker van 100 milliseconde (ms) gevolgd door een slotmedeklinker van 150 ms, terwijl een klinker van 200 ms wordt gevolgd door een medeklinker van 100 ms. Anders gezegd, het lijkt erop dat er sprake is van een compensatiemechanisme dat er voor zorgt dat als de klinker 100 ms langer duurt de slotmedeklinker 50 ms korter wordt. Bij de sprekers uit Orkney en Edinburgh is dit compensatiemechanisme een stuk zwakker: een toename van 100 ms in klinkerduur resulteert in een afname van 30 ms in slotmedeklinkerduur. Bij de Noorse sprekers zien we dat als de klinker 100 ms langer duurt, de medeklinker 60 ms korter wordt. Deze resultaten lijken dus aan te tonen dat het Shetlands in ieder geval wat betreft de lettergreepstructuur iets dichter bij het Noors ligt dan bij het Schotse Engels. Tevens blijkt dat het Orcadian zijn Scandinavische lettergreep-structuur heeft verloren.

In hoofdstuk 4, 5 en 6 staat de spraakmelodie van de twee dialecten centraal. In een reeks van proeven hebben we onderzocht of de intonatie van het Orcadian en het Shetlands inderdaad sterk van elkaar verschilt, en zo ja, op welke punten de twee intonatiesystemen dan precies van elkaar afwijken.

Hoofdstuk 4 had tot doel om na te gaan in hoeverre de bewoners van Orkney en Shetland in staat zijn de twee dialecten op basis van de intonatie van elkaar te onderscheiden. De proefpersonen kregen korte spraak-fragmenten te beluisteren van sprekers uit Orkney, Shetland en Edinburgh met als opdracht om op een antwoordformulier aan te geven of men dacht dat de spreker 'van het eigen eiland' of 'van elders' afkomstig was. In de eerste helft van het experiment kreeg men (via elektronisch ingrijpen) dusdanig onverstaanbaar gemaakte spraak te horen dat het aan de spraakklanken niet meer was vast te stellen waar de spreker vandaan kwam; de spraakmelodie werd hierbij in tact gelaten. Zodoende zijn we er zeker van dat de luisteraars hun beslissing nemen uitsluitend op basis van de intonatie van de spraakfragmenten. In de tweede helft van het experiment was de spraak wel gewoon verstaanbaar. De uitkomst van de serie experimenten kan als volgt worden samengevat. In het geval van de *onverstaanbare* spraak identificeren de luisteraars uit Orkney alle spraakfragmenten van sprekers uit Orkney als 'van het eigen eiland' en classificeren ze de spraak uit Shetland en Edinburgh als 'van elders'. Voor de Shetlandse luisteraars zien de resultaten er iets anders uit. Spraak uit Orkney wordt als 'van elders' geïdentificeerd en spraak van Shetlanders als 'van het eigen eiland'. Spraak van sprekers uit Edinburgh wordt echter óók als 'van het eigen eiland' geclassificeerd. Deze uitkomst suggereert op dat er een overeenkomst is tussen de intonatie van Shetland en die van Edinburgh, terwijl de intonatie van het Orcadian kennelijk anders is. In het geval van de *verstaanbare* spraak kunnen de luisteraars uit zowel Orkney als Shetland de sprekers van het eigen eiland moeiteloos onderscheiden van de sprekers van de andere eilandgroep of uit Edinburgh. Hieruit concluderen we dat de klanken in de drie taalvariëteiten sterk en kenmerkend verschillen.

Om vast te kunnen stellen op welke punten de twee intonatiesystemen van elkaar afwijken hebben we in hoofdstuk 5 een analyse gemaakt van de melodie van de twee eilanddialecten. Daartoe hebben we geluidsopnames gemaakt van een veertigtal sprekers die elk een aantal zinnetjes voorlazen van het type *There are many gardens in Bergen* en *Are there many gardens in Bergen*? Het resultaat van de intonatieanalyse brengt drie verschillen aan het licht. Ten eerste spreken zowel de mannen als de vrouwen uit Orkney op een gemiddeld hogere toonhoogte dan de Shetlanders. Ten tweede vinden we een verschil in locatie van de accentverlenende toonhoogtebeweging, de 'toonpiek'. ten opzichte van de beklemtoonde lettergreep waar deze piek bij hoort. In het Shetlands valt deze piek samen met de beklemtoonde lettergreep, oftewel op de eerste lettergreep van *many*, *gardens* en *Bergen*. Dit is het patroon zoals we dat vinden in de meeste Engelse dialecten (inclusief die van oostelijk Schotland) en in het Nederlands. In het Orcadian is de piek een flink stuk naar achteren verschoven zodat hij terechtkomt op de onbeklemtoonde (tweede) lettergreep. Soortgelijke late pieken komen ook voor in sommige Scandinavische talen maar ook in Keltische talen (Welsh, Iers en Gaelic). De gevonden piekverschuiving hangt waarschijnlijk samen met het derde verschil dat we hebben geconstateerd, namelijk dat in het Orcadian de duur van de eerste lettergreep relatief korter is dan in het Shetlands. Een statistische analyse van de meetresultaten geeft aan dat de pieklocatie akoestisch gezien verreweg het belangrijkste, d.w.z. meest onderscheidende, intonatieverschil is tussen de twee dialecten.

In hoofdstuk 6 hebben we een detailstudie uitgevoerd naar het effect van pieklocatie en gemiddelde toonhoogte op de herkenning van Orcadian en Shetlands door sprekers van deze dialecten. Net als in hoofdstuk 4 hebben we daarbij gebruik gemaakt van verstaanbare en onverstaanbare spraak. Bovendien hebben we het intonatiepatroon op een aantal manieren (elektronisch) gemanipuleerd. Naast gemonotoniseerde spraakfragmenten, kregen de luisteraars spraak te horen met vroege pieken (op de eerste lettergreep), met late pieken (op de tweede lettergreep) of met pieken tussen vroeg en laat in. Tevens hebben we de gemiddelde toonhoogte gemanipuleerd: gemiddeld relatief hoog (als in het Orcadian) tegenover gemiddeld laag (als in het Shetlands). De serie van manipulaties werd uitgevoerd zowel op een spraakfragment met Orkney als een met Shetland spraakklanken. Zo kregen de proefpersonen dus bijvoorbeeld Shetlandse spraak te horen met vroege pieken, maar ook met late pieken, zoals je die in het Orcadian vindt. In het tweede geval is de intonatie dus 'Orcadian' terwijl de klinkers en medeklinkers Shetlands zijn. De proefpersonen dienden wederom aan te geven of ze dachten dat de spreker 'van het eigen eiland' of 'van elders' afkomstig was. In grote lijnen is de uitkomst van deze experimenten als volgt. In het geval van de *onverstaanbare* fragmenten vinden de Shetlandse luisteraars dat spraak met een relatief lage toonhoogte 'Shetlandser' klinkt dan spraak met een relatief hoge toonhoogte; de luisteraars uit Orkney lijken geen speciale voorkeur voor een bepaalde toonhoogte te hebben. De locatie van de toonpiek speelt geen rol van betekenis bij het bepalen van de herkomst van de spreker. In het geval van de *verstaanbare* spraak vinden we als uitkomst dat Shetlandse luisteraars spraak met vroege pieken (op de eerste lettergreep), ongeacht de toonhoogte, als het 'meest Shetlands' beoordelen terwijl luisteraars uit Orkney spraak met late pieken (op de tweede lettergreep) het 'meest Orcadian' vinden klinken. Deze uitkomst lijkt dus aan te tonen dat de pieklocatie inderdaad het belangrijkste kenmerk is waarin de twee dialecten van elkaar verschillen.

De belangrijkste conclusie van dit proefschrift is dat de dialecten van Orkney en Shetland zowel wat betreft hun lettergreepstructuur als spraakmelodie van elkaar verschillen. Deze conclusie roept meteen de volgende vraag op: wat is de oorsprong van deze verschillen? Op het eerste gezicht lijkt het antwoord tamelijk voor de hand te liggen, namelijk dat we in het hedendaagse Shetlands meer terugvinden van het Norn dan in het Orcadian. Zo blijkt dus het Shetlands zijn oorspronkelijke Scandinavische lettergreepstructuur tot op zekere hoogte te hebben behouden terwijl het Orcadian op dit punt niet afwijkt van het Schots. Anders gezegd, het dialect van Shetland is wat minder 'verschotst' dan het Orcadian; dit contrast vinden we ook terug in andere uitspraakverschillen tussen de twee dialecten.

Het opvallendste verschil tussen de twee dialecten, de afwijkende intonatie, laat zich daarentegen aanmerkelijk minder makkelijk verklaren. Zoals eerder gezegd wordt er vaak beweerd dat de opmerkelijke intonatie van het Orcadian 'Scandinavisch' zou zijn. Inderdaad lijken er overeenkomsten te zijn tussen het Orcadian en talen als het Deens en het Zweeds – deze talen hebben eveneens late toonpieken. Het is echter merkwaardig dat er nu juist bij het 'verschotste' Orcadian sprake zou zijn van Scandinavische intonatie maar niet bij het nauwer aan het Scandinavisch verwante Shetlands. Er is evenwel wellicht een andere verklaring voor de herkomst van de intonatieverschillen. In de Keltische talen en in het door het Keltisch beïnvloede Engels zoals dat gesproken wordt in Wales, Noord Ierland en Glasgow vinden we ook relatief late toonpieken. Aangezien in het noorden van Schotland tot voor kort eveneens een Keltische taal, namelijk het Gaelic, werd gesproken zou het dus ook mogelijk zijn dat het Orcadian zijn spraakmelodie heeft overgenomen van die taal.[55] Een vervolgonderzoek waarbij de intonatie van het Orcadian en het Shetlands systematisch wordt vergeleken met de intonatie van Noorse en Keltische dialecten zal in de toekomst meer duidelijkheid moeten brengen in deze kwestie.

---

[55] Een paar procent van de bevolking van de Schotse Hooglanden spreekt nog steeds Gaelic, de rest spreekt nu Highland English.

Summary in English

Viking invaders from Norway arrived in Orkney and Shetland – groups of islands to the north of mainland Scotland – in the first half of the ninth century. What happened to the indigenous people after the arrival of the Vikings is unclear although it has been variously claimed that the natives were either assimilated, driven out or exterminated. The Scandinavian language spoken by the colonisers and their descendants became known as Norn, and this was to remain the chief medium of communication for several centuries. In 1468 Orkney and in 1469 Shetland were pledged to Scotland by King Christian I of Denmark and Norway, as security for his daughter's dowry on her marriage to the future James III of Scotland. The dowry itself was never paid, and this is how the islands became a Scottish province. After the annexation, Scottish administrators and landowners, bringing with them the Scots language, began to arrive in Orkney and Shetland. Through a process of language shift, Norn gradually became increasingly restricted to the family circle, and in the course of the eighteenth century it was finally replaced by Lowland Scots.

The substratal influence of Norn on the present-day dialects of Orkney and Shetland is, however, apparent not only in the vocabulary and the grammar but also in the pronunciation. Catford (1957a) has pointed out that Shetland dialect seems to have preserved a typically Scandinavian syllable structure, implying that monosyllabic words ending in a consonant generally contain either a short vowel followed by a long consonant (as in *pott*), or a long vowel followed by a short consonant (as in *boat*). A similar inverse relationship between vowel and consonant duration is to be found in Norwegian and Swedish. Moreover, according to popular belief, there are affinities in intonation (i.e. speech melody) between Orkney speech and varieties of Norwegian. Note that this does not hold true for Shetland, and in fact there appears to be a striking dissimilarity in intonation between the two dialects. Impressionistically, Orcadian is characterised by very distinctive, 'lilting' patterns, whereas Shetland speech is relatively low pitched, with somewhat level intonation. Up till now, to our knowledge, no work appears to have been published on investigations of Orkney or Shetland intonation, nor have any contrastive studies of the two varieties been produced.

Chapter 3 of this dissertation aims to establish whether present-day Shetland dialect has preserved its inverse relationship between vowel and final consonant duration mentioned above, and to investigate whether a similar pattern is to be found in Orcadian. In addition, for comparison, an examination was undertaken of vowel and consonant duration in Scottish Standard English and Norwegian. Audio recordings were made of (in total) 36 native speakers from Shetland, Orkney, Edinburgh and south-west Norway. Each informant was asked to read a list of approximately a hundred monosyllabic words, e.g. *deep*, *big* and *time*. The list also included about twenty Shetland, Orkney or Edinburgh dialect words matched to the native variety of the speakers; the Norwegian participants were presented with a similar list of Norwegian words. So as to obtain uniform reading speed, each item was embedded in the sentence *I say ... again* (*jag sa ... alltid* for Norwegian). Computerised measurements of vowel and consonant duration of the target words yielded the following results.

1. For Shetland it was found that when the vowel duration was 100 milliseconds (ms), final consonant duration was 150 ms, whereas a relatively long vowel of 200 ms was followed by a consonant of 100 ms in duration. In other words, there was a considerable degree of compensation in final consonant duration, making up for changes in vowel duration, with a 100 ms change in vowel duration resulting in an inverse change in consonant duration of 50 ms.

2. In Orkney and Edinburgh speech this compensatory mechanism was found to be significantly weaker. In these varieties, an increase in vowel duration of 100 ms resulted in a decrease of ca. 30 ms in final consonant duration.

3. In the case of Norwegian, a 100 ms change in vowel duration was reflected by an inverse change in final consonant duration of ca 60 ms.

These results indicate that, at least with respect to the inverse relationship between vowel and final consonant duration, Shetland is linguistically somewhat closer to Norway than to Central Scotland. Furthermore, it would seem that Orkney dialect has lost its Scandinavian syllable structure.

Chapters 4, 5 and 6, which are all concerned with the speech melody of the two dialects, report on a series of experiments carried out to investigate the validity of impressionistic claims for intonational differences between Orkney and Shetland dialects. Chapter 4 examines the extent to which Orkney and Shetland speakers are able to identify their own dialect purely on the basis of intonation. Listeners from both island groups were asked to judge short fragments of speech recorded by male speakers hailing from Orkney, Shetland and Edinburgh. The listeners were required to indicate on a response sheet whether they thought a particular speaker was 'from their own island' or 'from elsewhere'. In the first part of the experiment, the speech sound was electronically modified so that all that remained of the speech signal was the rhythm and melody. Having thus rendered recognition of individual vowels and consonants impossible, listeners would be forced to try to identify the language variety solely on intonation. After the participants had listened to the unintelligible speech, the same fragments were then repeated (in a different order) as normal, intelligible speech. The outcome of these experiments revealed that, in the case of the *unintelligible* speech, listeners from Orkney identified Orkney speech as 'from their own island', while speech from Shetland and Edinburgh was classified as 'from elsewhere'. The results for the Shetland listeners were quite different: although they correctly identified Orkney speakers as being 'from elsewhere', and Shetland speech as 'from their own island', Edinburgh speech was also categorised as 'from their own island'. These findings suggest that there are similarities between Shetland and Edinburgh intonation, whilst Orkney dialect has a distinctly different speech melody. In the case of the *intelligible* speech, neither Orkney nor Shetland listeners had any difficulty in distinguishing the three language varieties. Consequently, one may assume that there are clear differences between Orkney, Shetland and Edinburgh with respect to vowel and consonant pronunciation.

The aim of Chapter 5 was to determine the characteristic features of the intonation systems of the two dialects. Recordings were made of a total of 39 Orkney and Shetland speakers, each reading sentences of the type *There are many gardens in Bergen* and *Are there many gardens in Bergen?* The recordings were transferred to computer and the intonation patterns were then displayed on computer screen. Three major differences were observed between the two dialects.

1. It emerged that, for both male and female speakers, the overall pitch level in Orkney was substantially higher than in Shetland.

2. A significant difference was found regarding the location of the pitch peak relative to the stressed syllable with which it is associated. In Shetland, the pitch peak coincides with the stressed syllable, namely it is located on the first syllable of *many*, *gardens* and *Bergen*. So, in Shetland rises in pitch typically occur at the beginning of most words. Such a pattern is typical of the intonation of the vast majority of mother-tongue English speakers (including those of eastern Scotland) and is also found in many other languages – to give just one example, Dutch. In Orkney, however, the pitch peak occurs much later in the word, so that the peak is located on the *unstressed* syllable, i.e. on the second syllable of *many*, *gardens* and *Bergen*. In other words, in Orcadian rises tend to occur towards the end of words. In language, late pitch peaks are

relatively unusual, but they do indeed feature in certain Scandinavian languages, and also in Celtic languages, such as Welsh, Irish, and possibly also Scots Gaelic.

3.   Finally, it was found that the difference in pitch-peak location seemed to have an effect on the duration of the stressed syllable, with Orkney dialect having relatively shorter first syllables (i.e. stressed), than does Shetland speech. The outcome of a statistical analysis of the results indicated that pitch-peak location is the most important difference between Orkney and Shetland.

Chapter 6, reports on a detailed study of the effect of pitch-peak location and overall pitch level on the identification of Orkney and Shetland speech by native speakers of the two varieties. For this investigation, the original intonation pattern of the recorded speech was electronically manipulated in various ways. Using special speech-processing software, a range of different test sentences was synthesised, with the pitch peaks occurring either early (on the first syllable), late (on the second syllable) or at some intermediate point. In addition, the overall pitch level of the test sentences was altered, being rendered relatively high pitched (as in Orkney), or relatively low pitched (as in Shetland). The manipulations were applied to samples of unintelligible and intelligible speech originating from both Orkney and Shetland. Thus, listeners were presented with, for example, Shetland speech with early pitch peaks (as is normal for Shetland dialect), but also with late peaks (as is the case in Orkney). In the latter case, the intonation pattern is 'Orcadian' even though the vowels and consonants are pronounced by a Shetlander.

As in Chapter 4, listeners had to decide whether they thought a particular speaker was 'from their own island' or 'from elsewhere'. The results can be summarised as follows: in the case of *unintelligible speech*, Shetland listeners associate low pitch with speech 'from Shetland' and high pitch with speech 'from elsewhere', whilst participants from Orkney seem to make no such judgements. The location of the pitch peak played no role in the identification of the dialect of the speaker. In the case of the *intelligible* speech, it was found that, irrespective of the overall pitch level, Shetlanders regard early pitch peaks (on the first syllable) as 'most Shetland', while Orcadians consider late peaks (on the second syllable) to be 'most Orcadian'. These findings indicate that the difference between the two dialects is explained primarily by the location of the pitch peak.

The main conclusion of this dissertation is that the dialects of Orkney and Shetland, although closely related, exhibit remarkable differences both in terms of syllable structure and intonation patterns. The question then arises of what the origins and causes of these differences are. At first sight, there is an obvious answer, namely that Shetland retains more features attributable to the influence of Norn than does Orkney. For example, it is certainly true that Shetland has preserved its Scandinavian syllable structure, whereas that of Orkney is no different from Edinburgh speech. In this respect, one might say that Shetland dialect has become less 'Scottified' than Orcadian.

The difference in intonation between the two dialects is, nevertheless, harder to explain in these terms. As previously stated, it is often claimed that Orkney's lilting intonation is 'Norwegian'; and indeed, there do seem to be similarities in this regard between Orcadian and Scandinavian languages, like Danish, Swedish and, possibly also, Norwegian, which likewise have late pitch peaks. Yet, it is puzzling that one should find 'Scandinavian' intonation in Orkney, but not in Shetland dialect, even though the latter actually appears, in other respects, to be the more Scandinavian of the two. However, there may well be another explanation for the origin of the melodic differences. Late peaks are found not only in Celtic languages, but also crucially in varieties of English that have been *influenced* by a Celtic language – examples include broad Glasgow and Belfast varieties and much Welsh English. Gaelic was, until recently, the chief language of much of northern Scotland, and one possible explanation could be that Orkney intonation has been in some way affected by the various Gaelic-influenced mainland dialects.[56]

Further research is clearly required so as to provide a systematic comparison of the intonation patterns of Orkney and Shetland dialects with those found in northern Scottish English, including those of Celtic-influenced varieties, and also with the intonation patterns of Norwegian. This would enable linguists to establish more precisely the origins of the curious differences in the prosodic systems of Orkney and Shetland dialects.

---

[56] Today, Highland English is spoken by the overwhelming majority of the population of this region, with fewer than five per cent claiming to speak Gaelic.

Curriculum vitae

Klaske van Leyden werd op 1 mei 1959 geboren te Gouda. In 1988 behaalde zij de HBO propedeuse Engels aan de MO lerarenopleiding te Rotterdam. In 1990 met begon zij met de studie Engelse taal- en letterkunde aan de Universiteit Leiden. In 1992/1993 studeerde zij met een Hartingbeurs aan het Department of Linguistics van de Universiteit van Edinburgh waar zij zich specialiseerde in de fonetiek. In februari 1995 behaalde zij aan de Universiteit Leiden het doctoraaldiploma Engels op basis van een afstudeeronderzoek op het gebied van audio-visuele spraakperceptie uitgevoerd aan de Technische Universiteit Delft. Aansluitend werkte zij een half jaar als onderzoeksassistent op het Fonetisch Laboratorium van de Universiteit Leiden aan een onderzoek naar de rol van klemtoon bij de herkenning van gesproken woorden. Van 1999 tot 2004 werkte zij aan het onderzoek waar in deze dissertatie verslag van wordt gedaan, eerst naast een functie bij Koninklijke TPG Post, de laatste twee jaar als parttime onderzoeker in dienst van de Universiteit Leiden.

Acknowledgements

It is truly a pleasure for me to have this opportunity of thanking all the people of Orkney and Shetland who have assisted me in the course of this research. As anyone who has undertaken linguistic fieldwork will confirm, this type of investigation would have been quite impossible without such co-operation. So many people helped in so many different ways, and I am able to mention only a few individuals by name.

Firstly, I shall always be grateful to Brian Smith (Shetland Archives) for the many exchanges in which we discussed historical issues, for his willingness to share with me his unrivalled knowledge of local history, and also for his frankness in debunking much of the too commonly believed "Norn myth". My thanks also go out to Billy Scott (Orkney College), Ian Tait (Shetland Museum) and the staff of BBC Radio Orkney, all of whom went to great efforts in helping me to find informants, and provided much more in the way of advice and assistance. In addition, I want to place on record my gratitude to all my (necessarily anonymous) Orkney and Shetland informants for their patience, kindness, encouragement and good humour – not to mention dozens of very welcome cups of tea and countless biscuits. Finally, special thanks go to Nan Scott, who consistently provided me with a home-from-home whenever I was doing fieldwork in Orkney.

Possibly some Orkney and Shetland friends and acquaintances may have felt that this research commitment was merely a good excuse for me to spend a part of my time each year in the Northern Isles – a place which I have grown to appreciate and love. They wouldn't be totally wrong!